Diet recommendations for TCM - Kidney - Yang deficiency

Please check these recommendations always with a TCM nutrition consultant, therapist, doctor or dietician. The recipes and the list of ingredients are supporting also the conventional medical therapy. The calorie disclosures of fresh ingredients (fruit and vegetables) vary according to quality and time of harvest. The contents were checked by a dietician and a nutrition consultant for the Traditional Chinese Medicine (TCM).

Author:
©2017 Josef Miligui
www.ebns.at

Source:
The lists are created from the EBNS database for nutritional counseling. The database is used by dietitians, therapists and doctors for advising the patient / client.

Literature:
The specialist literature and the training documents of the German and Austrian dietary and traditional Chinese medicine serve as a knowledge base. We have used the documents as a basis of knowledge, adapted it to our experience and completed them.
http://di-book.com

Title Photo:
©2008 Erika Weixlbaumer

Production and publishing:
BoD – Books on Demand, Norderstedt
ISBN: 9783752861396

Diet recommendations for TCM - Kidney - Yang deficiency

1 Treatment strategy

Tonify and warm Yang, strengthen middle, warm.
Hot - LITTLE, warm and neutral YES, refreshing LITTLE, cold NO.

2 Avoid

All cold, raw food, tropical fruits, black and green tea, dairy products, yoghurt, indigestible, sugar !!!, sweets, soft drinks, cocktails, sauna, sweating, wheat beer.

3 Breakfast

4 Snack

5 Lunch

6   Afternoon

7   Dinner

8   Any time

9 Recipes

(recommendable) = You can use more.
(little) = You should use less than specified or omit.

9.1 8 treasures of rice

Strengthens kidney and bladder, builds up Qi, strengthens the spleen, repels moisture, reduces internal heat, prevents cancer, builds heart, calms nerves.
Cooking time approx. 1 hour
Calories p. portion: 212
4 portions

Quantity of ingredients

Lily bulbs 1 table spoon / 5g. (recommended)...................................*
Longane 1 table spoon / 5g. (little)......................................*
King Solomon's-seal 1 table spoon / 5g. (recommended)..................*
Yam root, yam root tuber 1 table spoon / 5g. (recommended)...........*
Coix (seeds) YiYi Ren 1 table spoon / 5g. (yes)...............................*
Rice wild (nature rice) 1 1/2 cups / 240g. (recommended)..........metal
Water 8-10 cups / 800g. (yes) .... earth

Cooking instructions:

Each one 1 tbsp: Bai He, Longan, Yu Zhu, Da Zao, Shan Yao, Lian Mi, Yi Yi Ren, Qian Shi
Add hot water and soak for about 30 minutes. Then add 1 - 2 cups of rice (normal) and simmer for 1/2 to 1 hour until the rice is very soft. Or: Cook for about 3 hours with the herbs a congee. Then the herbs do not have to be soaked.

9.2 Barley mash with steamed pear

Moisturizes lungs, cools heat, reduced hot lung mucus, produces humors, moisturizes, relaxes, builds up Qi, spreads, forces spleen, cools bladder, diuretic, moisturizes intestines, relaxes, builds up Qi, spreads.
Cooking time approx. 25 min
Calories p. portion: 114
5 portions
Allergens: A

Quantity of ingredients
Water 10 cups / 1200g. (yes)... earth
Barley 1 cup / 120g. (yes)... earth
Ginger fresh 2 slices / 2g. (recommended) ....metal
Cardamom 3 capsules / 1g. (recommended) ....*
Salt 1 pinch / 1g. (recommended)..water
Pear 1 piece / 200g. (yes) .... earth
Sugar cane sugar 1/2 teaspoon / 5g. (little) .... earth

Cooking instructions:
Grind coarse the barley and roast it dry. Add hot water, add ginger and cardamom and let it swell to a pulp in low heat. Peel and dice the pear and boil for 10 minutes with a little water. At the end, add the stewed pear, a little butter and sweetener.

Variant: If you want to go fast, you can use barley flakes instead of shot.

9.3   Barley soup

Works neutral to slightly warming and relaxes the Qi flow. Helps with loss of appetite and diarrhea due to spleen weakness. With weak spleen qi, one should often eat salty soups for breakfast.
Cooking time approx. 25 min
Calories p. portion: 265
2 portions
Allergens: A

Quantity of ingredients
Barley 1 cup / 120g. (yes)... earth
Salt 1 pinch / 1g. (recommended)..water
Ginger fresh 1/2 teaspoon / 1g. (recommended)........................metal
Olive oil 1 table spoon / 10g. (yes)... earth
Parsley 2 table spoons / 30g. (recommended)...........................wood
Water 1 1/2 cups / 240g. (yes)... earth

Cooking instructions:
Roast the barley in the pan, then grind it to the ground, and boil with water, some salt and ginger to a mash. Before serving add oil and parsley.

Variant: You can add a better taste to the dish if you cook it with prepared vegetable or meat broth.

9.4   Basic recipe for a beef broth (clear)

Strengthens Qi and Yang, is very warming.
Cooking time approx. 4-8 hours
Calories p. portion: 114
10 portions
Allergens: O

Quantity of ingredients

Beef soup meat 1,1 lbs / 500g. .... earth
Beef meatbones 5/8 oz / 200g. .... earth
Vinegar (Red wine vinegar) 1 dash / 3g. .... wood
Juniper berry 8 pieces / 6g. .... fire
Rosemary 1 pinch / 1g. .... fire
Carrot 3 pieces / 210g. .... earth
Parsnip 2 pieces / 300g. .... fire
Leek 1 piece / 200g. .... metal
Ginger fresh 1/2 teaspoon / 5g. .... metal
Lovage 1 stem / 15g. .... metal
Clove 2 pieces / 2g. .... metal
Pimento 6 pieces / 12g. .... metal
Anise (Common Fennel) 2 pieces / 1g. .... earth
Salt 1 teaspoon / 5g. .... water
Water 3,3 lbs / 1300g. .... earth

Cooking instructions:
Heat water, a dash of red wine vinegar, some juniper berries, a little
rosemary, bones and meat till it boils; add carrot, parsnip, leek, ginger,
lovage, clove, allspice, star anise and a little salt; simmer for 4-8 hours
then strain.
Refrigerate for later use.

9.5   Basic recipe for a chicken broth worming

Strengthens Qi and blood, is very warm.
Cooking time approx. 2-3 hours
Calories p. portion: 90
9 portions
Allergens: L

Quantity of ingredients

Chicken meat 1/2 piece / 600g. .... wood
Carrot 2 pieces / 150g. .... earth
Leek 1 stick / 45g. .... metal

Celery root 1 piece / 500g. .... earth
Ginger fresh 2 slices / 2g. ....metal
Fenugreek (Trigonella foenum-graecum) 1 teaspoon / 2g. ....*
Juniper berry 1 teaspoon / 3g. .... fire
Bay leaf 3 pieces / 2g. ....*
Water 4 cup / 900g. .... earth

Cooking instructions:

Remove chicken parts from fat. Place chicken pieces in a saucepan with hot water and heat till it boils briefly, skimming any resulting foam. Add coarsely chopped vegetables and all spices and cook over medium heat for 2 to 3 hours. Strain the finished soup. Throw away vegetables and bones.
Tip: If you want to use the meat as a soup insert, take out after 45 minutes and return only the bones in the soup.
Refrigerate for later use.

9.6   Basic recipe for a duck broth

Forces Qi, strengthens blood and fluids, nourishes Yin, forces stomach, cools heat, strengthens spleen and liver.
Cooking time approx. 2-3 hours
Calories p. portion: 61
6 portions
Allergens: L

Quantity of ingredients

Duck (heart) 5/8 oz / 200g. .... wood
Water 2 cup / 450g. .... earth
Duck (slaughtered) 1/4 lbs - 4oz / 100g. .... wood
Carrot 2 pieces / 100g. .... earth
Celery root 1/2 piece / 600g. .... earth

Cooking instructions:

Cook duck pieces with vegetables for 2-3 hours. Sift broth through a fine sieve and refrigerate for later use.

The innards can be reused: You cut them finely and leaves them for a few minutes with fresh vegetables in the broth draw. Sprinkle with parsley before serving.

9.7 Basic recipe for a fish broth

Strengthens kidney Qi and Yin, strengthens blood and fluids, promotes urination.
Cooking time approx. 40 min
Calories p. portion: 128
5 portions
Allergens: DLO

Quantity of ingredients
Fish pieces mixed (fresh water) 3/4 lbs / 300g. ....water
Celery root 1/4 lbs - 4oz / 120g. .... earth
Leek 2 inches / 10g. ....metal
Carrot 2 pieces / 150g. .... earth
White wine 1/2 cup / 125g. .... wood
Lemon 1/2 piece / 50g. .... wood
Bay leaf 2 leaves / 2g. ....*
Peppercorns 3 pieces / 2g. ....metal
Olive oil 1 table spoon / 10g. .... earth
Water 2 cup / 450g. .... earth

Cooking instructions:
Fry celery, chopped carrots and leeks in olive oil, add bay leaf and peppercorns, add pieces of fish and sauté briefly. Add water, add little white wine or lemon. Simmer gently for 30 minutes. Skim off the resulting foam several times. In the end, sift the ingredients through a cloth.
Refrigerate for later use.

9.8 Basic recipe for a reissue soup (Congee)

Warms the stomach and spleen, harmonizes the intestine, forces Qi, reduces moisture.
Cooking time approx. 2-4 hours
Calories p. portion: 140
3 portions
Allergens:

Quantity of ingredients
Rice variety any 1 cup / 120g. ....metal
Water 6 cups / 700g. .... earth

Cooking instructions:

Cook rice and water in a ratio of about 1: 6. The amount of water determines the thickness of the mash (matter of taste).

Put the rice in a saucepan with a heavy lid. It is important to simmer the rice after a short boil on the slightest flame, otherwise it burns.

Boil the rice for 2-4 hours. The longer he cooks, the more he strengthens.

If you want to eat the dish for breakfast, you can put the rice on just before bedtime.

To be on the safe side, you should first check the behavior of your pot and cooker under observation for a similar amount of time, so that nothing burns.

Refrigerate for later use.

9.9   Basic recipe for a vegetable soup, nutritious

Strengthens spleen and lung, regulates Qi flow, builds up Qi, dries out, passes downwardly, strengthens stomach Qi.

Cooking time approx. 2-3 hours
Calories p. portion: 48
5 portions
Allergens: L

Quantity of ingredients

Olive oil 1 table spoon / 4g. .... earth
Onion white 1 piece / 60g. ....metal
Carrot 3 pieces / 200g. .... earth
Parsnip 3/8 lbs - 6oz / 150g. .... fire
Celery root 1 cup / 100g. .... earth
Ginger fresh 1/2 teaspoon / 2g. ....metal
Lemon 1/2 piece / 25g. ....wood
Juniper berry 6 pieces / 6g. .... fire
Thyme dried 1 pinch / 1g. ....metal
Lovage 1 table spoon / 3g. ....metal
Bay leaf 2 leaves / 1g. .... *
Salt 1 pinch / 1g. ....water
Water 3 cups / 650g. .... earth

Cooking instructions:

Cut the vegetables into cubes.

Heat oil in hot pot, fry shortly onions and vegetables.

Add cold water, then add ginger, bay leaf and lemon juice.

Season with juniper, thyme and lovage. Cover for 2 - 3 hours on a low heat and simmer.
The used vegetables should be thrown away.
The basic recipe serves as a soup base and to refine vegetables, legumes or cereals.
If you want to eat vegetable soup immediately, add the desired vegetables half an hour before.
Refrigerate for later use.

9.10 Beef soup with carrots, leeks, bay leaves

Strengthens spleen Qi, strengthens blood and Qi, moisturizes, relaxes, builds up Qi, spreads, strengthens spleen and liver, regulates Qi flow, strengthens stomach Qi.
Cooking time approx. 2-3 hours
Calories p. portion: 194
5 portions

Quantity of ingredients
Beef meat 1 lbs / 500g. (recommended) .... earth
Carrot 2 pieces / 200g. (yes) .... earth
Leek 1/2 piece / 150g. (recommended) ....metal
Bay leaf 3 leaves / 1g. (recommended) ....*
Corn Grease (Polenta) 1 table spoon / 10g. (yes)...................... earth
Water 2 cup / 450g. (yes)... earth
Salt 1 pinch / 0,5g. (recommended)...water

Cooking instructions:
In a saucepan with water (enough to cover the meat), add beef soup meat or leg slice and simmer for a moment; then pour off the broth, rinse the meat with hot water (this will save you from foaming), clean the pot and put the meat in hot water again; add chopped carrot, leek, corn and bay leaf; simmer until the meat is cooked.

9.11 Black-eyed beans stew

Strengthens spleen and kidney, is very nutritious, warms the stomach and spleen, harmonizes the intestine, forces Qi, strengthens stomach and kidney, strengthens spleen and kidney.
Cooking time approx. 20 min
Calories p. portion: 140
5 portions

Quantity of ingredients
Black-eyed peas 1 cup / 100g. (yes)...water
Rice variety any 1 1/2 cups / 200g. (yes) ....metal
Water 10 cups / 1000g. (yes)... earth

Cooking instructions:
Soak the beans overnight and strain.

In a ratio of 1: 2, simmer the beans together with the rice in the Water. Depending on how hot the flame is and how thin the dish should be, more water must be added.

Variation: Add vegetables fried in oil, such as carrots, celery tubers, onions or leeks.

9.12 Boiled fillet with potatoebiscuits (Austrian Tafelspitz)

Strengthens spleen Qi, strengthens blood and Qi, moisturizes, relaxes, builds up Qi, spreads, forces Qi, forces spleen, relieves inflammation, moisturizes.
Cooking time approx. 3 hours
Calories p. portion: 454
8 portions
Allergens: L

Quantity of ingredients
Onion white 1 piece / 50g. (recommended)................................metal
Corn germ oil 1 table spoon / 10g. (recommended) .... earth
Water 32 cup - 1 gallon / 0g. (yes)... earth
Beef meat 5,4 lbs - 70oz cap of rump / 1800g. (reco.)................ earth
Beef meatbones 4n slices with bone marrow / 0g. (reco.) .... earth
Salt 1 pinch / 0,5g. (recommended)..water
Peppercorns 15 pieces / 0g. (little) ....metal
Parsnip 1 piece / 0g. (recommended)... fire
Carrot 2 pieces / 0g. (yes) .... earth
Celery root 1 slice / 0g. (recommended) .... earth
Parsley root 2 pieces / 0g. (recommended)................................... earth
Leek 1/2 stick / 0g. (recommended)..metal
Chives 1 table spoon (chopped) / 7g. (little)...............................metal
Potato 2,2 lbs / 1000g. (yes)... earth
Sunflower oil 2 table spoons / 20g. (yes) .... earth
Salt 1 pinch / 0,5g. (recommended)..water

Cooking instructions:
Halve the onions, but do not peel. Brown onions in a pan with fat on the cut surfaces very dark. Wash meat and bones briefly with warm water, drain.
Heat the water till it boils, put in meat and cook gently. Always scoop up rising foam. As soon as no more foam rises, add peppercorns and the onion. Clean and cut root and leeks and add after about two and a half hours cooking time. Simmer for another half hour.
Remove boiled beef from the soup, pour through a sieve and season with salt. Cut roots into bite-sized pieces. Add the soup together with the marrow bones and leave it under the boiling point. Cut the boiled beef into finger-
thick slices against the grain, place in the soup, heat again, sprinkle with a little chives.
In addition, cook and peel the potatoes in salted water. Stomp roughly or cut finely. Fry in a pan with the oil crispy.

9.13 Carrot and rice gruel soup

Warms the stomach and spleen, harmonizes the intestine, forces Qi, reduces moisture, strengthens spleen and liver, regulates Qi flow, moisturizes, relaxes, builds up Qi, spreads.
Cooking time approx. 10 min
Calories p. portion: 101
1 portions

Quantity of ingredients
Basic recipe for a rice soup (Congee) 1 cup / 120g. (reco.)...............*
Carrot 2 pieces / 100g. (yes) .... earth
Salt 1 teaspoon / 4g. (recommended)...water

Cooking instructions:
Peel and grate carrots. Heat the rice soup (according to the basic recipe) till it boils and add the grated carrots and salt. Cook for 10 minutes.

9.14 Celery juice

Strengthens stomach Qi, moisturizes, relaxes, builds up Qi, spreads.
Cooking time approx. 5 min
Calories p. portion: 33
1 portions
Allergens: L

Quantity of ingredients

Celery root 1/2 piece / 200g. (recommended) .... earth
Water 1 cup / 120g. (yes) .... earth
Salt 1 pinch / 0,5g. (recommended) .... water

Cooking instructions:
Peel celeriac and cut into pieces and juice. Mix with water and salt as needed.

9.15 Celery soup

Refreshing, builds up fluids and Qi.
Cooking time approx. 45 min
Calories p. portion: 101
4 portions
Allergens: ACGL

Quantity of ingredients

Water 2 cup / 500g. (yes) .... earth
Butter organic 1 table spoon / 15g. (yes) .... earth
Nutmeg 1 pinch / 1g. (yes) .... metal
Salt 1 pinch / 1g. (recommended) .... water
Spelled wholemeal flour 2-3 teaspoons / 25g. (yes) .... wood
Celery root 1 piece / 500g. (recommended) .... earth
Chicken egg 1 piece / 55g. (yes) .... earth
Cream sour 10% 2 table spoons / 25g. (recommended) .... *
Celery sticks 2 table spoons / 20g. (recommended) .... earth
Pepper (ground) 1 pinch / 0,5g. (little) .... metal

Cooking instructions:
In a hot saucepan, melt 1 tbsp butter; add a pinch of nutmeg, a pinch of salt, 1/2 cup wholegrain spelled flour (finely ground as fresh as possible) and stir to a sweat while stirring; add 1/2 liter of hot water gradually; add 1 large finely chopped celery tuber; cook for about 35 minutes and then puree; mix 1 egg yolk with 1 cup of cream; in the hot - no longer boiling! - soup vigorously; add some celery leaves finely chopped; with pepper, salt to taste.

9.16 Chicken soup with angelica root and buckthorn fruit

Strengthens spleen and nourishes the blood and Yin of the liver, forces Qi and blood, is very warming.
Cooking time approx. 1 1/2 hours
Calories p. portion: 77
3 portions
Allergens: LO

Quantity of ingredients
Basic recipe for a chicken soup 2 cup / 500g. (recommended) ....*
Angelica root 1/8 oz / 5g. (recommended) ....*
Bocksdorn fruits, goji berry dried 1/8 lbs - 2oz / 50g. .... wood

Cooking instructions:
When you cook chicken broth according to basic recipes add angelica root and Bocksdorn fruits in the last 40 minutes.

Ingestion: Drink 2-3 cups of broth daily.

9.17 Chicken soup with egg yolk and parsley

Forces Qi and blood, is very warming, nourishes blood and liver, harmonizes liver and spleen, forces eyesight, preserves the fluids, contracts.
Cooking time approx. 10 min
Calories p. portion: 118
2 portions
Allergens: CL

Quantity of ingredients
Basic recipe for a chicken soup 2 cup / 500g. (recommended) ....*
Chicken yolk 1 piece / 10g. (yes)... earth
Parsley 1 table spoon / 10g. (recommended)............................. wood

Cooking instructions:
Cook the chicken broth according to the basic recipe.
Heat broth and bubble the egg yolk. Sprinkle the chopped parsley over it and let it rest for about 2 minutes. Drink in small sips.

9.18 Chicken soup with green spelt, parsley and sake

Forces Qi and blood, is very warming, nourishes liver-blood, preserves the fluids, contracts, scatters and move Qi, moisturizes, reduces cold-evil, softens knots.
Cooking time approx. 1 1/2 hours
Calories p. portion: 150
2 portions
Allergens: AL

Quantity of ingredients
Basic recipe for a chicken soup 2 cup / 500g. (recommended) ....*
Green spelt 4 table spoons / 30g. (recommended) .... wood
Parsley 2 table spoons / 14g. (recommended)........................... wood
Sake 1 dash / 2g. (little)..metal

Cooking instructions:
Cook the chicken broth according to the basic recipe. Add the ingredients in the soup and simmer 10 min.

9.19 Chickpeas with Raisins

Strengthens spleen and liver, regulates Qi flow, moisturizes, relaxes, builds up Qi, spreads, strengthens spleen and heart, softens, passes downwardly, warms the stomach and spleen, harmonizes the intestine, forces Qi, reduces moisture.
Cooking time approx. 45 min
Calories p. portion: 429
2 portions
Allergens: EGO

Quantity of ingredients
Chickpeas 1 cup / 120g. (recommended) .... water
Hijiki 1 table spoon / 7g. (recommended)..................................water
Salt 1 pinch / 0,5g. (recommended)..water
Sunflower oil 1 table spoon / 10g. (yes) .... earth
Carrot 2 pieces / 160g. (yes) .... earth
Raisins 2 table spoons / 18g. (little) .... earth
Ginger fresh 1/2 teaspoon / 2g. (recommended)........................metal
Cumin (Caraway seed) 1 pinch / 0,2g. (little) ....metal
Lemon juice 1 dash / 1g. .... wood
Sour cream 15% fat 1 table spoon / 8g. ....*
Curcuma 1 pinch / 0,2g. .... *
Soybean milk 1 dash / 1g. (yes) .... earth

Coriander 1 pinch / 0,2g. (recommended)..................................metal
Soy sauce 1 dash / 1g. ....water
Rice round grain 1/2 cup / 60g. (yes)..metal
Water 3 cups / 250g. (yes) .... earth
Salt 1 pinch / 1g. (recommended)..water

Cooking instructions:
Preparation:
Soak chickpeas in cold water for several hours or overnight.

After that:
Pour soaking water away; put the chickpeas in cold water; Add 1 tbsp
Hijiki and cook the chickpeas bite-proof; Add salt at the end of the
cooking time.

Separately:
In a hot pan, fry oil, chopped carrots (more than chickpeas), raisins,
grated ginger, plenty of cumin and salt until the carrots are half cooked;
add the chickpeas and sea algae; Add lemon juice, a little sour cream,
turmeric, soy or rice milk; a pinch of cilantro, add some soy sauce; Let it
soak for a few minutes over low heat until the carrots are cooked.

Put the round grain rice with the water, salt and cook for about 20
minutes.

9.20 Clear ox tail soup with buckthorn fruit

Forces Qi, nourishes the liver blood, good for ocular fibrillation or dry
eyes, muscle tension or calf cramps due to blood deficiency.
Cooking time approx. 1-2 hours
Calories p. portion: 217
6 portions
Allergens: O

Quantity of ingredients
Basic recipe for a beef soup 4 cup / 1000g. (recommended)..............*
Beef Oxtail pieces 1,1 lbs / 500g. (recommended)...................... earth
Shiitake, dried 4-5 pieces / 4g. (yes).. earth
Onion white 1 piece / 60g. (recommended)................................metal
Sake 2 table spoons / 20g. (little)..metal
Ginger fresh 1/2 teaspoon / 2g. (recommended)........................metal
Bocksdorn fruits, goji berry dried 1 table spoon / 8g. .... wood

Cooking instructions:
Soak shiitake mushrooms. Blanch oxtail slices (This removes fat and impurities).
Cook in the beef broth for 1-2 hours.
Then add the spring onions, shiitake mushrooms, rice wine, buckthorn fruits and ginger and simmer gently.

9.21 Clear soup from goose

Forces spleen, stomach and lungs, relieves weakness, forces Qi, calms the stomach, gets Qi moving, directs upwards, strengthens spleen and liver, regulates Qi flow, moisturizes, relaxes, builds up Qi, spreads.
Cooking time approx. 2-3 hours
Calories p. portion: 334
6 portions

Quantity of ingredients
Goose parts 1,1 lbs / 500g. (yes)..metal
Carrot 1 piece / 100g. (yes)... earth
Onion (shallot) 1 piece / 25g. (recommended) ....metal
Leek 1 piece / 250g. (recommended) ....metal
Parsley 1 Twig / 4g. (recommended) ....wood
Lovage 1 Twig / 4g. (recommended) ....metal
Chervil 1 pinch / 0,2g. (recommended) ....*
Water 4 cup / 1000g. (yes) .... earth
Salt 1 pinch / 0,5g. (recommended)..water

Cooking instructions:
Simmer goose pieces with vegetables and herbs for 2-3 hours. Sift through a fine cloth and cool. Degrease and store in the refrigerator.

9.22 Coconut soup

Forces Qi and blood, is very warming, nourishes Yin, blood and Jing, moisturizes, relaxes, builds up Qi, spreads, gets Qi moving, directs upwards, dissolves stagnation.
Cooking time approx. 20 min
Calories p. portion: 153
6 portions
Allergens: L

Quantity of ingredients

Olive oil 2 table spoons / 20g. (yes)... earth
Leek 1 piece / 200g. (recommended) ....metal
Onion white 1 small / 40g. (recommended)................................metal
Basic recipe for a chicken soup 4 cup / 1000g. (recommended).........*
Lime 1/2 juice / 20g. (recommended)..wood
Coconut flakes 2 table spoons / 18g. (little) .... earth
Coconut milk 1 cup / 250g. (little)... earth
Pimento 1 pinch / 0,2g. (little) ....metal
Salt (herbal) 1 pinch / 1g. (recommended)................................water
Lemongrass 1 table spoon / 8g. (recommended)..............................*

Cooking instructions:

Pour olive oil into a pan, sauté the leek and onion, add the chicken broth, add the lemon grass, simmer for about 15 minutes, add coconut flakes and coconut milk, allspice and chilli, salt with herb salt. Garnish with lemongrass.

9.23 Compote of pears

Forces lung Qi. Ideal as a cure in the fall.
Cooking time approx. 10 min
Calories p. portion: 122
4 portions

Quantity of ingredients

Water 1 cup / 280g. (yes) .... earth
Pear 4 pieces / 800g. (yes).. earth
Anise (Common Fennel) 1/2 teaspoon / 1g. (recommended) ..... earth
Vanilla pod 1 pinch / 1g. (recommended)...*
Cocoa 1 pinch / 1g. (recommended)... fire

Cooking instructions:

Boil pears (organic - with peel), aniseed, vanilla, chili soft. Sprinkle with cocoa.

9.24 Corn coffee with cardamom

Dries out, passes downwardly.
Cooking time approx. 5 min
Calories p. portion: 3
1 portions

Quantity of ingredients

Cereal coffee 1 table spoon / 15g. (recommended)........................ fire
Cardamom 2 cores / 1g. (recommended) ....*
Water 1 cup / 120g. (yes).. earth

Cooking instructions:
Boil water, coffee, sugar and cardamom. Let it set for one min before drinking.

9.25 Grilled salmon steaks with cauliflower and potatoes

Forces Qi, spleen and blood, builds up Qi, forces kidneyn Yang.
Cooking time approx. 30 min
Calories p. portion: 330
4 portions
Allergens: D

Quantity of ingredients

Garlic 1 clove / 1g. ....metal
Onion (shallot) 1/2 piece / 5g. (recommended) ....metal
Lemon juice 1 dash / 1g. ....wood
Salt 1 pinch / 1g. (recommended)..water
Cauliflower 1 piece / 500g. (yes)... earth
Olive oil 2 table spoons / 20g. (yes)... earth
Garlic 1 clove / 1g. ....metal
Water 2/3 cup / 50g. (yes) .... earth
Parsley 2 table spoons / 15g. (recommended) ....wood
Potato 1,1 lbs / 500g. (yes).. earth
Salt 1 pinch / 1g. (recommended)..water
Salmon 4 pieces (steaks) / 500g. (recommended) ....water
Lemon 1/2 piece / 2g. .... wood

Cooking instructions:
Garlic shallots mixture:
Finely squeeze the garlic, finely chop the shallots, add a dash of lemon juice and salt and stir. Mix with a little oil to a paste.

Cauliflower:
Cut the cauliflower into pieces.
Heat the oil in a heavy saucepan and fry the crushed garlic for a short time.
Add the cauliflower pieces and turn in the oil. Add a little water and cook

until the cauliflower is firm. Strain the cauliflower and cook the remaining water until a thick sauce remains. Add the cauliflower and crush it roughly with a wooden spoon. Add the chopped parsley and salt.

Potatoes:
Cook the potato in a saucepan with plenty of water, strain and peel.

Salmon Steak:
Preheat the oven at about 180°C/356°F. Rub in the salmon slices with the garlic-scarlet mixture and grill as close as possible to the heat source for 4 to 8 minutes from both sides. You are done when the meat is easy to divide when you pierce with a fork.

Serve and sprinkle with lemon slices and the chopped parsley.

9.26 Hearty polenta mash

Strengthens spleen and stomach, promotes urination, harmonizes liver-Qi.
Cooking time approx. 10 min
Calories p. portion: 262
2 portions

Quantity of ingredients
Corn Grease (Polenta) 1 cup / 120g. (yes) .... earth
Onion (spring onion) 2 pieces / 40g. (recommended)................. metal
Ginger fresh 1/2 teaspoon / 2g. (recommended)........................ metal
Nutmeg 1 pinch / 1g. (yes) .... metal
Salt 1 pinch / 1g. (recommended)... water
Olive oil 1 table spoon / 10g. (yes).. earth
Turmeric (yellow root) 1 pinch / 1g. (recommended) .... *
Water 1 1/2 cups / 240g. (yes)... earth

Cooking instructions:
Stir in the polenta in boiling water and let it swell for 7 min. Add green onion, grated ginger, turmeric, nutmeg, salt and olive oil and wait for 3 more minutes.

9.27 Kidney bean pot with lamb and sage

Nourishes Yin from heart and kidney, strengthens spleen and kidney Yang, forces Qi, heats middle and lower heater, dissolves stagnation, directs upwards, moisturizes, relaxes, builds up Qi, spreads.
Cooking time approx. 1 1/2 hours
Calories p. portion: 391
4 portions
Allergens: F

Quantity of ingredients
Soybean oil 2 table spoons / 30g. (recommended) .... earth
Onion white 2 pieces / 120g. (recommended).............................metal
Lamb meat 5/8 oz / 200g. (recommended) .... fire
Salt 1 pinch / 0,5g. (recommended)...water
Sage 4-5 leaves / 2g. (yes)... fire
Rosemary 1/2 teaspoon / 2g. (recommended) .... fire
Thyme 1/2 teaspoon / 2g. (recommended) ....*
Kidney beans (red) 5/8 lbs - 8oz / 250g. (recommended)...........water
Water 3 cups / 750g. (yes) .... earth

Cooking instructions:
Soak kidney beans in water overnight and strain.
In a saucepan with oil, roast the onion. Dice the lamb and place in the pot.
Season with salt, sage, rosemary and thyme.
Roast lamb well and cover pot. Cook over low heat and add ten-quarters of a gallon (750ml.) of cold water after 10 minutes.
Salt again.
Heat till it boils. Add beans to it.
Simmer for at least 1 hour until the beans and meat are tender.

9.28 Kohlrabi Potatoes mash

Moves Qi and blood, reduces moisture, forces Qi, forces spleen, relieves inflammation, moisturizes, relaxes, builds up Qi, spreads, forces kidney Jing.
Cooking time approx. 25 min
Calories p. portion: 278
1 portions
Allergens: CG

Quantity of ingredients

Kohlrabi 1/2 piece / 150g. (recommended) .... earth
Potato 1/4 lbs - 4oz / 100g. (yes) .... earth
Butter organic 1 table spoon / 10g. (yes) .... earth
Chicken yolk 1 piece / 25g. (yes) .... earth

Cooking instructions:

Remove the kohlrabi leaves, wash the tuber and tender leaves and the
potatoes thoroughly. Peel the kohlrabi and potatoes, cut into cubes
about 1 cm in size. Melt half the butter in a small saucepan, add the
kohlrabi and the potatoes and fry in it. Steam with 2 tablespoons of
water in a closed saucepan over low heat for about 15 minutes.
Meanwhile, free the tenderest kohlrabi leaves from the stems and chop
very finely. In total, at most 2 tablespoons of leaf pieces should be
used. Add this to the vegetables about 5 minutes before the end of the
cooking time. Stir in the egg yolk and bring to the boil again. Put the
vegetables in a plate and mix with the remaining butter and egg yolk.
(Crush for the baby with a fork.)

9.29 Lentils and rice stew

Strengthens spleen and liver, regulates Qi flow, moisturizes, relaxes,
builds up Qi, spreads, warms the stomach and spleen, harmonizes the
intestine, forces Qi, reduces moisture, brings the liver Qi in motion,
cools heat.
Cooking time approx. 25 min
Calories p. portion: 232
3 portions
Allergens: LNO

Quantity of ingredients

Lentils 1/4 lbs - 4oz / 100g. (recommended) .... water
Water 5 cups / 500g. (yes) .... earth
Rice variety any 1 cup / 120g. (yes) .... metal
Sesame oil 1 table spoon / 10g. (yes) .... earth
Carrot 2 pieces / 150g. (yes) .... earth
Celery sticks 2 rods / 20g. (recommended) .... earth
Cumin (Caraway seed) 1 pinch / 0,2g. (little) .... metal
Salt 1 pinch / 0,5g. (recommended) .... water
Vinegar (Apple vinegar) 1 dash / 2g. (little) .... wood
Parsley 2 table spoons / 18g. (recommended) .... wood

Cooking instructions:
Soak the dry lentils the day before.
Heat sesame oil in a hot pot; cut carrot and celery into small pieces and sauté; add rice, a pinch of cumin and lentils and heat till it boils.
If the lenses are soft, add salt; season with a little vinegar and garnish with parsley.

Variant: In summer you can omit the cumin and add fresh green peas, Chinese cabbage or celery.

9.30 Millet with egg and butter

Forces blood, Yin and Jing, nourishes Yin, moisturizes in case of internal dryness, forces blood, forces spleen, calms nerves and stomach, strengthens spleen and kidney, diuretic, strengthens Qi and kidney Jing, moisturizes, relaxes, builds up Qi, spreads.
Cooking time approx. 25 min
Calories p. portion: 338
2 portions
Allergens: CG

Quantity of ingredients
Millet 1 cup / 100g. (yes) .... earth
Ginger fresh 1/2 teaspoon / 1g. (recommended)........................metal
Salt 1 pinch / 0,5g. (recommended)...water
Parsley 2 table spoons / 16g. (recommended)...........................wood
Pepper powder (hot) 1 pinch / 1g. (recommended) .... fire
Chicken egg 2 pieces / 100g. (yes).. earth
Butter organic 2 table spoons / 20g. (yes)................................ earth
Nutmeg 1 pinch / 0,2g. (yes)..metal
Water 1 1/2 cups / 200g. (yes).. earth

Cooking instructions:
Simmer the millet with the ginger and nutmeg in the water for 5 min. and let it swell for another 30 min.
Cook and peel 1 soft egg per person; pile up the millet on plates and place 1 egg each in a hollow in the millet mountain; Put butterflakes over it. Sprinkle with chopped parsley and the rose paprika.

9.31 Nettle-chard soup

Drains moisture down, strengthens blood, cools liver heat.
Cooking time approx. 30 min
Calories p. portion: 52
4 portions

Quantity of ingredients
Nettles Handful / 10g. (recommended) .... wood
Chard 1 lbs / 500g. (recommended) .... earth
Salt 1 pinch / 1g. (recommended) .... water
Water 2 cup / 400g. (yes) .... earth
Olive oil 1 table spoon / 10g. (yes) .... earth
Pepper (ground) 1 pinch / 0,5g. (little) .... metal

Cooking instructions:
Heat the oil in a saucepan, add the washed and finely chopped Swiss chard. Salt and let simmer for 10 minutes. Add the chopped nettles and cook for another 10 minutes. Add pepper and puree.

9.32 Oat Congee

Forces Qi, forces liver and spleen, moisturizes intestines, eliminates mucus, holds back sweat.
Cooking time approx. 2-4 hours
Calories p. portion: 162
3 portions
Allergens: A

Quantity of ingredients
Oat 1 cup / 125g. (recommended) .... metal
Water 6 cups / 700g. (yes) .... earth

Cooking instructions:
Cook oats and water in a ratio of about 1: 6. The amount of water determines the thickness of the mash (pure matter of taste). The oats swell, so do not take much. Put the oats in a saucepan with good insulation and a heavy lid. It is important to simmer the oats after a short boil on the slightest flame, otherwise it burns. Cook the oat for 2-4 hours. The longer it cooks, the more he strengthens.

9.33 Oatmeal soup with spring onion and carrots

Strengthens spleen and liver, regulates Qi flow, moisturizes, relaxes, builds up Qi, spreads, moisturizes intestines, regulates Qi, warms spleen and kidney, dissolves stagnation, directs upwards.
Cooking time approx. 30 min
Calories p. portion: 135
3 portions
Allergens: AG

Quantity of ingredients
Oat 6 table spoons / 48g. (recommended)................................metal
Carrot 2 pieces / 200g. (yes)....................................... earth
Butter organic 1 table spoon / 15g. (yes) .... earth
Nutmeg 1 pinch / 1g. (yes) ....metal
Lovage 1 stem / 15g. (recommended) ....metal
Onion (spring onion) 2 pieces / 40g. (recommended)................metal
Water 2 cup / 480g. (yes)... earth

Cooking instructions:
Roast the oats in butter, add salt and spices, pour in water and heat till it boils. After 10 min. add the grated carrots and lovage, cook for 10 minutes. Finely add chopped onion.

9.34 Oyster mushrooms with asparagus

Tonifies lungs and kidneys Yin, balances heat, dissipates moisture.
Cooking time approx. 30 min
Calories p. portion: 316
4 portions
Allergens: GH

Quantity of ingredients
Onion white 1 piece / 50g. (recommended)................................metal
Butter organic 2 table spoons / 40g. (yes)................................. earth
Oyster mushroom 3/4 lbs / 300g. (yes)...................................... earth
Sake 2 table spoons / 40g. (little)................................metal
Parsley 2 table spoons / 40g. (recommended)........................... wood
Walnuts 2 table spoons / 60g. (little)................................ earth
Asparagus (green or white) 1,1 lbs / 500g. (little)....................... earth
Salt 1 pinch / 1g. (recommended)................................water
Sugar white 1 pinch / 0,1g. (little)................................ earth
Potato 1 lbs / 500g. (yes)... earth
Salt (herbal) 1 pinch / 1g. (recommended)................................water

Cooking instructions:
Cook organically grown potatoes with the skin, otherwise prepare peeled boiled potatoes. Boil the asparagus in salted water with a pinch of sugar and salt. (You can cook an old roll that absorbs the bittering substances.) Slightly sauté the chopped onions in a pan in the butter before frying the oyster mushrooms cut into the same pan. Stew 15 minutes, stirring several times. Add the sake, walnuts and parsley and simmer on low heat while you drain the potatoes and asparagus. Finally, sprinkle some herbal salt over it.
If no fresh asparagus is available, asparagus can be used in jars.

9.35 Pumpkin curry

Forces lungs and spleen, diuretic, forces Qi, protects liver, warms the stomach and spleen, harmonizes the intestine, forces Qi, reduces moisture, moisturizes, relaxes, builds up Qi, spreads, nourishes blood and liver, harmonizes liver and spleen.
Cooking time approx. 20 min
Calories p. portion: 193
3 portions

Quantity of ingredients
Pumpkin 3/4 lbs / 300g. (recommended) .... earth
Olive oil 2 table spoons / 30g. (yes).. earth
Coriander 1 pinch / 1g. (recommended)....................................metal
Pepper (ground) 1 pinch / 0,5g. (little).......................................metal
Curry 1 pinch / 1g. (recommended) ....metal
Water 1/4 cup / 50g. (yes) .... earth
Salt 1 pinch / 1g. (recommended)...water
Parsley 1 table spoon / 7g. (recommended)..............................wood
Cardamom 1 pinch / 1g. (recommended)...*
Turmeric (yellow root) 1 pinch / 1g. (recommended) ....*
Rice (whole grain) 1/2 cup / 60g. (yes) ....metal
Water 3 cups / 300g. (yes) .... earth
Salt 1 pinch / 1g. (recommended)...water

Cooking instructions:
Heat olive oil in pan. Steam the pumpkin cut in cubes, season with cilantro, pepper and curry, simmer with a little water, salt with sea salt,

add chopped parsley with cardamom and turmeric, simmer on a small fire for about 10 minutes, depending on the pumpkin, the pumpkin should still be firm.

Place the rice in salted water, bring to the boil and let it simmer over low heat for about 15 minutes.

9.36 Pumpkin soup

Forces lungs and spleen, diuretic, forces Qi, protects liver, forces Qi, forces spleen, relieves inflammation, moisturizes, relaxes, builds up Qi, spreads, strengthens spleen and liver, regulates Qi flow, moisturizes, relaxes, builds up Qi, spreads.
Cooking time approx. 1 hour
Calories p. portion: 105
3 portions

Quantity of ingredients
Pumpkin 3/4 lbs / 300g. (recommended) .... earth
Carrot 2 pieces / 100g. (yes) .... earth
Potato 2 pieces / 120g. (yes) .... earth
Olive oil 1 table spoon / 10g. (yes) .... earth
Onion white 1 piece / 50g. (recommended) ....metal
Water 1 cup / 120g. (yes) .... earth
Parsley 1 table spoon / 7g. (recommended) .... wood
Anise (Common Fennel) 1 pinch / 1g. (recommended) .... earth
Salt 1 pinch / 1g. (recommended) ....water

Cooking instructions:
Add the olive oil to the pan, add the diced pumpkin, diced carrots and potatoes. Roast them shortly, add the finely chopped onion, fill with water, add enough water to cover the vegetables at least 3 finger-widths. Boil at low heat.

Season with sea salt, add small cutted parsley, a pinch of anise (little). Allow to simmer for about 35 minutes. Then purée the soup and add some water, depending on the consistency of the soup.

9.37 Quick flakes with compote or jam

Forces Qi, dries out, passes downwardly, strengthens middle heater, moisturizes, relaxes, builds up Qi, spreads, strengthens kidney Qi, essence and brain, forces kidney, warms the middle.
Cooking time approx. 5 min
Calories p. portion: 189
2 portions
Allergens: H

Quantity of ingredients
Quinoa 5-7 table spoons / 50g. (recommended) .... fire
Water 1 cup / 250g. (yes) .... earth
Compote (fruits of the season) 1 cup / 100g. (recommended) .... *
Walnuts 1 table spoon (grated) / 8g. (little) .... earth
Olive oil 1 table spoon / 10g. (yes) .... earth
Honey 2 table spoons / 20g. (little) .... earth
Vanilla 1 pinch / 0,2g. (yes) .... *
Anise (Common Fennel) 1 pinch / 0,2g. (recommended) .... earth
Cardamom 1 pinch / 0,2g. (recommended) .... *

Cooking instructions:
Put the quinoa flakes in a pan and add water. Boil for 3-5 minutes, pull from the fire, add nuts and compote. Add a dash of oil. Sweeten as needed with honey, whole cane sugar or agave syrup.

Spices and aromas: vanilla, anise, fennel or coriander, cardamom, a little chili.

Winter: apple compote, pear compote, fruit jam.
Summer: plum compote, apricot compote.

9.38 Quick zucchini soup

Reduces mucus, preserves the fluids, cools liver fire, forces stomach Qi.
Cooking time approx. 10 min
Calories p. portion: 42
4 portions

Quantity of ingredients
Zucchini 2-3 pieces / 500g. (recommended) .... earth
Onion white 1 piece / 50g. (recommended)................................metal
Corn germ oil 2 table spoons / 6g. (recommended).................... earth
Parsley 1 table spoon / 7g. (recommended)..............................wood
Chives 1 teaspoon / 3g. (little) ....metal
Water 2 cup / 400g. (yes)... earth

Cooking instructions:
Fry chopped onion in oil. Add sliced zucchini and sauté well. Pour with water. Chop parsley and chives, add and puree everything.

9.39 Quinoa with peach

Strengthens blood and fluids, brings blood into motion, builds up Qi, spreads, forces Qi, dries out, passes downwardly, strengthens middle heater, moisturizes.
Cooking time approx. 20 min
Calories p. portion: 248
2 portions

Quantity of ingredients
Quinoa 1 cup / 100g. (recommended) .... fire
Water 1 1/2 cups / 240g. (yes)... earth
Honey 2 teaspoons / 4g. (little)... earth
Peaches 2 pieces / 240g. (little).. earth
Linseed oil 2 teaspoons / 4g. (recommended) .... earth
Lemon Balm (fresh) 1 teaspoon (chopped) / 1g. (reco.) ....metal
Cinnamon ground 1 pinch / 0,2g. (recommended) ....*
Vanilla 1 pinch / 0,2g. (yes) ....*

Cooking instructions:
In the evening: Put quinoa in hot water and boil soft, covered 15 to 20 minutes.
In the morning: Warm up quinoa with 1 tablespoon water.
Steam lightly Peaches in a saucepan or add them fresh. Decorate with fresh lemon balm.

Summer: nectarines, apricots
Winter: Pickled fruit, pear, apples

9.40 Reissue soup with fresh fruits

Forces kidney and bladder, strengthens Qi and kidney Jing, moisturizes, relaxes, builds up Qi, reduces internal heat, produces humors, moisturizes, spreads, expels cold, dissolves stagnation, drives sweat, stimulates nerves.
Cooking time approx. 1 1/2 hours
Calories p. portion: 143
4 portions
Allergens: G

Quantity of ingredients
Rice wild (nature rice) 1 cup / 100g. (recommended) .... metal
Water 8 cups / 900g. (yes) .... earth
Apple (sweet) 1 1/2 cups / 200g. (yes)...................................... earth
Butter organic 1 table spoon / 10g. (yes) .... earth
Vanilla 1 pinch / 0,2g. (yes) .... *
Sugar cane sugar 2 teaspoons / 6g. (little)................................ earth

Cooking instructions:
Prepare rice congee according to basic recipe.

At the end, add finely chopped fruits to the season, vanilla, chili and butter; sweet to taste.

Variant: With nuts, the dish can always be made richer and more filling.

Effect: Cooked or steamed fruits are easier to digest and act better than raw. For some fruits, which are particularly suitable for hot summer days - such as melons and berries - it is still advisable to add the fruits only to a hot porridge.
Other types of fruit - such as apples, pears, plums and cherries - can also be simmered for a while.

9.41 Rice congee with carrots and fennel

Nutritious builds up Qi, forces the digestive functions.
Cooking time approx. 2 hours and more
Calories p. portion: 131
3 portions
Allergens: G

Quantity of ingredients

Basic recipe for a rice soup (Congee) 2 cup / 500g. (reco.).................*
Carrot 2 pieces / 100g. (yes) .... earth
Fennel 1 piece / 250g. (recommended) .... earth
Butter organic 1 teaspoon / 3g. (yes)... earth
Cardamom 1/2 teaspoon / 1g. (recommended)................................*

Cooking instructions:

Cook rice congee according to basic recipe.
Clean and cut carrots and fennel.

When carrots and fennel are cooked from the beginning, they serve wholesomeness. If added shortly before the end of the cooking time, taste and vitamins are retained.

Refine with butter and cardamom before serving.

9.42 Rice congee with crushed walnuts

Nourishing and slightly warming, warms the middle, builds up Qi, warms the stomach and spleen, harmonizes the intestine, forces Qi, reduces moisture.
Cooking time approx. 2 hours and more
Calories p. portion: 406
2 portions
Allergens: H

Quantity of ingredients

Basic recipe for a rice soup (Congee) 4 cups / 500g. (reco.).............*
Sugar cane sugar 2 table spoons / 20g. (little)............................ earth
Walnuts 1 cup / 70g. (little).. earth
Cinnamon ground 1 pinch / 0,2g. (recommended) ....*

Cooking instructions:

Cook the basic recipe for rice soup (congee)
Note: The crushed walnuts can be cooked from the beginning.
Variation: Refine with sweet or spicy ingredients as you like. In particular, cinnamon, cloves, and ginger increase the warming effect and wholesomeness.

9.43 Rice congee with dried fruit

Warms the stomach and spleen, harmonizes the intestine, forces Qi, reduces moisture, nourishes blood and Yi, harmonizes lungs Qi, strengthens Qi and kidney Jing, moisturizes, relaxes, builds up Qi, spreads.
Cooking time approx. 10 min
Calories p. portion: 210
2 portions
Allergens: GO

Quantity of ingredients
Basic recipe for a rice soup (Congee) 4 cups / 500g. (reco.).............*
Butter organic 1/2 teaspoon / 5g. (yes)...................................... earth
Apricot dried 6 table spoons / 50g. (recommended).................... earth
Water 1/2 cup / 50g. (yes)... earth
Maple syrup 1 dash / 3g. (yes) .... earth

Cooking instructions:
Cook rice congee according to basic recipe.

Melt a small amount of butter over a low heat and briefly fry small dried fruit with 1/2 cup of water. Add the amount of rice porridge desired for the meal and heat. Serve hot and sweeten with maple syrup if necessary.
Variant: In addition fresh fruit with braise.

9.44 Rice congee with honey pear and black sesame

Especially good in kidney Yin deficiency, moisturizes lungs, cools heat, reduces lung mucus, produces humors, moisturizes, relaxes, builds up Qi, spreads, moisturizes intestines, nourishes Yin.
Cooking time approx. 10 min - 3 hours
Calories p. portion: 158
2 portions
Allergens: N

Quantity of ingredients
Basic recipe for a rice soup 1 1/2 cups / 240g. (recommended) ....*
Pear 2 pieces / 300g. (yes)... earth
Sesame, black 1 teaspoon / 3g. (recommended)....................... wood

Cooking instructions:
Cook rice congee according to basic recipe.
Fill pot with 3 cm of water and heat till it boils. Quarter the pears (with the skin and seeds) and simmer them covered with black sesame for 10 minutes. Mix with the rice.

9.45 Rice dulse soup

Strengthens spleen and liver, regulates Qi flow, relaxes, builds up Qi, spreads, dries out, passes downwardly, strengthens stomach Qi, warms the stomach and spleen, harmonizes the intestine, forces Qi, reduces moisture.
Cooking time approx. 5 min
Calories p. portion: 190
2 portions
Allergens: L

Quantity of ingredients
Basic recipe for a rice soup (Congee) 4 cups / 500g. (reco.) ....*
Basic recipe for a vegetable soup 2 cup / 500g. (recommended) ....*
Dulse (seaweed) 2 table spoons / 15g. (recommended) ....water

Cooking instructions:
Worm up a portion of pre-cooked basic recipe for a ricesoupe (congee) and a portion pre-cooked basic recipe for a vegetable soup.
Bake the dulse in the oven at 220 degrees for 3 minutes. Spread the crisp dulse over the rice.

9.46 Rice noodle soup with shiitake mushrooms

Strengthens spleen and liver, regulates Qi flow, relaxes, builds up Qi, spreads, dries out, passes downwardly, strengthens stomach Qi, nourishes Yin of the lungs, stomach and colon, supports digestion, reduces internal wind.
Cooking time approx. 20 min
Calories p. portion: 66
2 portions
Allergens: L

Quantity of ingredients
Rice noodles 2 handful / 20g. (yes) ....metal
Shiitake, dried 4-6 pieces / 5g. (yes).......................... earth
Basic recipe for a vegetable soup 1 1/2 cups / 240g. (recommended)*
Chinese cabbage 1 cup / 60g. (yes) .... earth

Lovage 1 teaspoon / 3g. (recommended) .... metal
Miso 2 table spoons / 18g. (recommended) .... water

Cooking instructions:
Soak rice noodles and shiitake mushrooms separately in cold water. Heat the vegetable broth and add the soaked shiitake mushrooms cut into strips and simmer gently. Cut Chinese cabbage into noodles, add lovage green and rice noodles and let it steep for a while. Before serving, stir in Miso dissolved in a little cooled water. Recommendation: Suitable at the beginning of each meal, also for breakfast

9.47 Rice porridge with shallots

Warms the stomach and spleen, harmonizes the intestine, forces Qi, reduces moisture, regulates Qi, warms spleen and kidney, dissolves stagnation, directs upwards.
Cooking time approx. 25 min
Calories p. portion: 177
2 portions

Quantity of ingredients
Rice variety any 1 cup / 100g. (yes)... metal
Water 4 cups / 400g. (yes) .... earth
Onion (spring onion) 2 table spoons / 12g. (recommended) .... metal

Cooking instructions:
Boil the rice with the water until a porridge is formed. Finely chop onion and keep for 5 min. to let go.

9.48 Rice with parsnips

Regulates Qi, dries out, passes downwardly, warms the stomach and spleen, harmonizes the intestine, forces Qi, reduces moisture. moisturizes, relaxes, builds up Qi, spreads. distributes mucus, activates Wei Qi, forces Qi.
Cooking time approx. 45 min
Calories p. portion: 206
3 portions

Quantity of ingredients

Rice variety any 1 cup / 120g. (yes)..metal
Water 1 1/2 cups / 200g. (yes)... earth
Salt 1 pinch / 1g. (recommended)...water
Parsnip 3-4 pieces / 450g. (recommended) .... fire
Olive oil 1 table spoon / 10g. (yes).. earth
Sage 1 teaspoon / 3g. (yes) .... fire

Cooking instructions:

Peel the parsnips and cut into slices. Fry for a short time in oil. Add the rice and fry again for a short time. Add the water and cook it at least 30 min. Sprinkle with fresh chopped sage.

9.49 Rice with stewed vegetables

Dissipates heat and moisture.
Cooking time approx. 20 min
Calories p. portion: 166
2 portions
Allergens: L

Quantity of ingredients

Rice variety any 1/2 cup / 60g. (yes)...metal
Water 3 cups / 300g. (yes) .... earth
Lemon peel 1 piece / 3g. (recommended)..................................... fire
Water 1/2 cup / 0g. (yes).. earth
Carrot 2 pieces / 180g. (yes) .... earth
Celery sticks 1/2 piece / 5g. (recommended) .... earth
Champignon 1/2 cup / 50g. (yes).. earth
Cress 2 table spoons / 20g. (little) ....metal
Linseed oil 1 dash / 3g. (recommended).................................... earth

Cooking instructions:

Cook rice according to basic recipe with a piece of lemon peel.
Steam chopped carrots, celery and mushrooms until soft.
Then sprinkle with cress. Then add a dash of high quality cold oil.

9.50 Roasted millet with Celery sticks

Strengthens spleen and kidney, diuretic, brings the liver Qi in motion, cools heat, moisturizes, relaxes, builds up Qi, spreads.
Cooking time approx. 30 min
Calories p. portion: 400
2 portions

Quantity of ingredients

Millet 1 cup / 120g. (yes) .... earth
Water 1 1/2 cups / 240g. (yes)... earth
Celery sticks 2 rods / 50g. (recommended)............................... earth
Herbs various 1 table spoon / 10g. (yes)..*
Water 2 table spoons / 30g. (yes)... earth
Salt 1 pinch / 1g. (recommended)...water
Sage 3-4 leaves / 2g. (yes).. fire
Cress 1 teaspoon / 3g. (little)..metal

Cooking instructions:
Roast millet briefly, pour over water, heat till it boils and let stand for 20 min. to swell.
Cut celery into small pieces and mix with water, salt and fresh herbs and cook for 10 min. Add to the millet. Sprinkle fresh sage or watercress over it.

9.51 Roasted nuts

Strengthens kidney Qi, essence and brain, forces kidney, builds up essence, warms lungs, moistens the intestine, moisturizes, relaxes, builds up Qi, spreads.
Cooking time approx. 5 min
Calories p. portion: 973
2 portions
Allergens: H

Quantity of ingredients

Hazelnuts 1/4 lbs - 4oz / 100g. (yes)... earth
Cashews 1/4 lbs - 4oz / 100g. (yes)... earth
Walnuts 1/4 lbs - 4oz / 100g. (little).. earth

Cooking instructions:
Roast nuts in a pan for about 5 minutes.

9.52 Roasted oatmeal with grapes compote

Moisturizes, relaxes, builds up Qi, spreads, forces Qi, warms the stomach and spleen, promotes blood circulation and conduction flow.
Cooking time approx. 25 min
Calories p. portion: 328
2 portions
Allergens: AO

Quantity of ingredients

Oat flakes roasted 1 cup / 120g. (yes) ....metal
Grapes red 1 1/2 cups / 240g. (little)... earth
Ginger fresh 1/2 teaspoon / 1g. (recommended).......................metal
Raisins 2 table spoons / 20g. (little) .... earth
Cinnamon ground 1 pinch / 1g. (recommended) ....*
Water 1 1/2 cups / 200g. (yes).. earth

Cooking instructions:

Roast the oats briefly, pour over water, add raisins and cook while stirring for 20 min. Add grapes, ginger and cinnamon.

9.53 Rosemary Potatoes

Forces Qi, forces spleen, relieves inflammation, relaxes, builds up Qi, spreads.
Cooking time approx. 30 min
Calories p. portion: 188
2 portions

Quantity of ingredients

Potato 6-8 pieces / 420g. (yes)... earth
Salt (herbal) 1 pinch / 1g. (recommended)..................................water
Olive oil 1 table spoon / 10g. (yes)... earth
Rosemary 1 teaspoon / 2g. (recommended)................................. fire

Cooking instructions:

Cut the potatoes into half´s, apply a little olive oil on the cut surface, then salt, sprinkle 2 - 3 rosemary needles on the potatoes.
Place the potatoes on the baking tray and bake them in the preheated oven for approx. 25 minutes to 190°C/374°F.

9.54 Russian kasha with white cabbage

Strengthens spleen stomach and intestine Qi, has a slightly warming effect.
Cooking time approx. 30 min
Calories p. portion: 250
2 portions
Allergens: AG

Quantity of ingredients
Buckwheat whole grain 1 cup / 130g. (recommended)...............wood
Water 1 1/2 cups / 240g. (yes)... earth
Nutmeg 1 pinch / 1g. (yes) ....metal
Salt 1 pinch / 1g. (recommended)...water
Parsley 1 table spoon / 10g. (recommended)............................wood
Ground 1 pinch / 2g. (recommended) .... earth
Butter organic 1 teaspoon / 3g. (yes).. earth
White cabbage Handful / 20g. (recommended)........................... earth

Cooking instructions:
Roast buckwheat golden yellow; add boiling water, heat till it boils
briefly and then let it swell until soft; Grate the white cabbage finely and
fold in. Season with nutmeg, a little salt; some parsley, cumin and butter
at the end.

9.55 Sake hot

Gets Qi moving, moisturizes, reduces cold-evil, softens knots.
Cooking time approx. 5 min
Calories p. portion: 0
1 portions

Quantity of ingredients
Sake 0,7 oz- 2cl / 2g. (little)...metal

Cooking instructions:
Heat sake and drink.

9.56 Scrambled eggs with rocket and herbs

Nourishing and slightly warming.
Cooking time approx. 10 min
Calories p. portion: 360
1 portions
Allergens: CG

Quantity of ingredients
Butter organic 2 table spoons / 20g. (yes).................................. earth
Ginger fresh 1 knife tip / 1g. (recommended).............................metal
Chicken egg 2 pieces / 120g. (yes).. earth
Pepper (ground) 1 pinch / 0,5g. (little)..metal

Coriander 1 pinch / 1g. (recommended)....................................metal
Parsley 2 table spoons / 16g. (recommended)...........................wood
Rucola 2 handful / 30g. (little)... fire
Oregano dried 1 teaspoon / 2g. (recommended).......................metal
Savory 1 pinch / 0,5g. (recommended) ....water

Cooking instructions:
Melt a piece of butter in a hot pan; add fine cutted ginger and roast it shortly. Mix in 1 egg whipped, pepper freshly ground, a pinch of coriander, bean cabbage, some salt, parsley chopped, rocket and oregano cut into small pieces until the egg stalls, but still juicy. Garnish: millet, polenta, potatoes, toasted bread. The dish is wholesome, without carbohydrate.

9.57 Tea from anise

Warms the middle, forces stomach and spleen, warms stomach, reduces cold-evil, harmonizes stomach-Qi, warms kidney.
Cooking time approx. 15 min
Calories p. portion: 3
4 portions

Quantity of ingredients
Anise (Common Fennel) 1 teaspoon / 3g. (recommended) .... earth
Water 2 cup / 500g. (yes) .... earth

Cooking instructions:
Heat the water till it boils and put it aside. Add anise.
10 min. to let go.
Pour through a tea strainer. Sweet to taste with honey.
In order to achieve a salutary effect, you should drink 2 cups of anise tea per day.

9.58 Tea from basil

Dries out, passes downwardly.
Cooking time approx. 10 min
Calories p. portion: 0
4 portions

Quantity of ingredients
Basil 1 teaspoon / 2g. (recommended) ....metal
Water 2 cup / 500g. (yes) .... earth

Cooking instructions:
Heat the water till it boils and put it aside. Add basil and 10 min. to let go. Sweet to taste with honey.

9.59 Tea from celery sticks

Brings the Liver Qi in motion, cools heat, moisturizes, relaxes, builds up Qi, spreads.
Cooking time approx. 15 min
Calories p. portion: 1
4 portions
Allergens: L

Quantity of ingredients
Celery sticks 2 table spoons (chopped) / 18g. (recommended) .. earth
Water 2 cup / 500g. (yes) .... earth

Cooking instructions:
Heat the water till it boils and put it aside. Add cutted celery and cook for 10 min. to let go. Strain. Sweet to taste with honey.

9.60 Tea from cinnamon sticks

Warms the stomach and spleen, promotes blood circulation and conduction flow, relieves cold-sickness and pain.
Cooking time approx. 15 min
Calories p. portion: 2
1 portions

Quantity of ingredients
Cinnamon sticks 1/4 piece / 1g. (recommended) ....*
Water 1 cup / 125g. (yes) .... earth

Cooking instructions:
A quarter of a cinnamon stick for a cup of tea. Start cold and bring to the boil. Let it sit for 15 minutes, then strain.
This tea is unsweetened and swallowed, slowly drunk. The amount is enough for one day.

9.61 Tea from fennel

Forces Yang, reduces cold-evil, harmonizes stomach-Qi.
Cooking time approx. 10 min
Calories p. portion: 0
4 portions

Quantity of ingredients
Fennel tea 2 table spoons / 20g. (recommended)...................... earth
Water 2 cup / 500g. (yes)... earth

Cooking instructions:
Heat the water till it boils and put it aside. Add fennel tea and 10 min. to
let go. Sweet to taste with honey. Strain when pouring.

9.62 Tea from ginseng

Forces heart, lungs, stomach, spleen, kidney-Qi.
Cooking time approx. 20 min
Calories p. portion: 0
4 portions

Quantity of ingredients
Ginseng 2 teabags / 4g. (recommended)..*
Water 2 cup / 500g. (yes)... earth

Cooking instructions:
A very mild form of taking ginseng is achieved by placing it in a thermos
of hot water. You can also use the root several times, not just for a pot
filling. Ideally, you should have cooked the water for 10 minutes - it is
then assigned to the conversion phase of fire (TCM) - and to use non-
carbonated medicinal spring water, if the quality of the water on site is
not good.

Ingestion: This mild ginseng tea can be drunk throughout the day for
strengthening.

9.63 Tea from ground

Reduces mucus and moist heat in the liver and gallbladder, against liver
Qi stagnation, spleen qi deficiency, spleen and kidney Yang-deficity.
Cooking time approx. 10 min
Calories p. portion: 2
4 portions

Quantity of ingredients
Ground 1 teaspoon / 3g. (recommended) .... earth
Water 2 cup / 500g. (yes) .... earth

Cooking instructions:
Heat the water till it boils and put it aside. Add crushed cumin and leave
for 10 min. to let go. Sweet to taste with honey. Strain when pouring.

Drink 1 cup 2 times a day.

9.64 Tea from rosemary

Dries out, passes downwardly, forces heart, lung and spleen Qi, forces
liver-blood, forces heart-Yin, expels spleen heat / cold moisture,
strengthens spleen and kidney Yang.
Cooking time approx. 15 min
Calories p. portion: 1
4 portions

Quantity of ingredients
Rosemary 2-4 teaspoons / 6g. (recommended) .... fire
Water 2 cup / 500g. (yes) .... earth

Cooking instructions:
Heat the water till it boils and put it aside. Add rosemary and 10 min. to
let go. Strain. Sweet to taste with honey.

9.65 Tea from thyme

Converts mucus, forces lungs and spleen, dries out, passes
downwardly.
Cooking time approx. 10 min
Calories p. portion: 0
4 portions

Quantity of ingredients
Thyme 3 table spoons / 6g. (recommended) .... *
Water 2 cup water / 500g. (yes) .... earth

Cooking instructions:
Heat the water till it boils and put it aside. Add thyme and 10 min. to let
go. Strain. Sweet to taste with honey.
Drink 2 to 3 cups daily by mouth

9.66 Tee Yogi tee

Reduces lung wind cold, forces kidney-Yang.
Cooking time approx. 20 min
Calories p. portion: 0
4 portions

Quantity of ingredients
Yogi tea 1 teabag / 2g. (recommended)....................................metal
Water 2 cup / 500g. (yes).. earth

Cooking instructions:
Boil the water and add the tea for 10-20 minutes. to let go. Yogi tea
consists of a spice mixture with cinnamon, cardamom, ginger, cloves
and black pepper. Since Yogi tea is very flavorful, you should use loose
tea rather sparingly or dose.

9.67 Thick pea soup

Nourishes Qi, diuretic, harmonizes Qi (especially in the Middle and
Lower), strengthens the kidney and the defense Qi, dischars moisture.
Cooking time approx. 2-3 hours
Calories p. portion: 123
3 portions
Allergens: AN

Quantity of ingredients
Peas, green 3/8 lbs - 6oz / 150g. (yes) ....water
Water 2 1/4 cups / 550g. (yes)... earth
Sesame oil 1 table spoon / 20g. (yes)... earth
Onion white 1/2 piece / 25g. (recommended)............................metal
Ginger fresh 1/2 teaspoon / 1g. (recommended).......................metal
Ground 1/2 teaspoon / 1g. (recommended) .... earth
Oat meal 1 table spoon / 15g. (recommended) ....metal
Salt 1 pinch / 1g. (recommended)...water
Parsley 1 stem / 2g. (recommended) .... wood

Cooking instructions:
Soak dried peas before cooking. Sauté sesame oil, onion, a little
oatmeal, ginger and cumin in a hot pot; add the peas and simmer for 2-
3 hours; add salt at the end and pruée with a blender; garnish with
parsley.

9.68 Tsampa with jam or fruit compote

Nourishes fluids, reduces stomach heat, forces spleen, produces essence, harmonizes stomach, moisturizes intestines.
Cooking time approx. 5 min
Calories p. portion: 280
1 portions
Allergens: AGO

Quantity of ingredients
Tsampa (roasted barley flour) 2 table spoons / 30g. (yes).......... earth
Water 6-8 table spoons / 70g. (yes)... earth
Butter organic 1/2 teaspoon / 2g. (yes)....................................... earth
Strawberry jam 1 table spoon / 7g. (recommended)....................wood
Sunflower seeds 2 teaspoons / 14g. (recommended) .... earth
Apple (sweet) 1 piece grated / 120g. (yes)................................. earth

Cooking instructions:
Pour tsampa with boiling water and stir with a spoon until a porridge is formed.
Add butter, jam, sunflower seeds and grated apple.
Sweet to taste with honey, whole cane sugar, or barley malt.
Spices and herbs: fresh mint, vanilla or cocoa, anise, cinnamon

Summer: jam or compote of your choice
Winter: nuts and apple or pear

9.69 Warming porridge

Forces Qi and defensive power.
Cooking time approx. 10 min
Calories p. portion: 357
1 portions
Allergens: AHO

Quantity of ingredients
Oat flakes (whole grain) 6 table spoons / 60g. (recommended)..metal
Fig dried 3 pieces / 15g. (yes) .... earth
Star anise 1 piece / 1g. (recommended) ....*
Ginger fresh 1 pinch / 0,5g. (recommended)..............................metal
Water 1 cup / 120g. (yes)... earth
Maple syrup 1 table spoon / 10g. (yes)...................................... earth
Walnuts 1 table spoon (chopped) / 8g. (little)............................. earth

Cooking instructions:
Soak the dried fruit. Roast Oatmeal dry. Add dried ginger, star anise or cinnamon, a little grated ginger and boil everything with water to a mash. With maple syrup sweet. Whip grated walnuts and sprinkle before serving.

Effect: Suitable for the cold season.
Caution: Fresh ginger does not drink over a long period of time.

10 Effects of food

10.1 Use ingredients: recommendable

Acai powder
Acerola fruit nectar or powder
Agar agar (kelp)
Agave nectar
Agrimony
Amaranth Pops
Anchovy / Sardine
Angelica root
Anise (Common Fennel)
Apple juice (natural cloudy)
Apple puree
Apricot dried
Apricot jam
Apricot nectar
Apricots juice
Baking powder
Banchatee (green tea)
barberry
Barley flour
Barley grass powder
Barley grouts
Barley malt
Basic recipe for a beef soup
Basic recipe for a beef soup (warming)
Basic recipe for a chicken soup (warming)
Basic recipe for a fish soup
Basic recipe for a rice soup (Congee)
Basic recipe for a vegetable soup (nutritious)
Basil
Basil (fresh)
Bay leaf
Beans (green, fresh)
Bearberry leaf
Beef bone marrow

Beef fillet
Beef heart
Beef heart (calf)
Beef kidney
Beef liver
Beef lungs (calf)
Beef meat
Beef meat (calf)
Beef meatbones
Beef Oxtail pieces
Beef soup meat
Beef stomach
Beer (alcohol-free)
Beer (alcohol-reduced)
Berries of the season
Bitter Herb liqueur
Bitter Lemon
Bitter liqueur
Bitter orange peel
Black beans
Black caraway
Black fungus mushroom
Blackberry dried (unripe fruit)
Blackberry jam
Blackberry leaves
Blackthorn (Sloe)
Blue mallow tee
Blueberry dried
Blueberry jam
Bocksdorn fruits (Fructus Lycii, Goji, goji berry dried
Borage
Boxhorn clover seeds
Brazil nuts
Bread roll
Bread with carob kernel flour

Breadcrumbs (wheat bread, bread roll)
Brie cheese
Broad beans (thick beans)
Brown ale
Brussels sprouts
Buckbean
Buckwheat whole grain
Bush beans
Butter (half fat)
Butter beans white
Calamari
Camembert
Campari
Capers in olive oil
Cardamom
Carob flour, St. john's bread
Celery root
Celery sticks
Cereal coffee
Chamomile tea
Channa-Dal
Chard
Chenpi (chinese tangerine bowl)
Cherry
Cherry (sour)
Cherry compote
Chervil
Chervil dried
Chestnut puree
Chicken Blood
Chicken egg white
Chickpeas
Chickweed
Chili (pod or ground)
Chinese pearl barley
Chocolate
Chocolate (Diabetic)
Chrysanthemum blossom tea
Cinnamon ground
Cinnamon sticks
Clarified butter
Clementine
Clove
Cocoa
Coconut fat
Coconut meat
Cod
Codfish
Cola drink
Cola drink (low calorie)
Compote (fruits of the season)
Coriander
Coriander (fresh)
Corn (fast polenta)

Corn (roasted)
Corn flour
Corn germ oil
Corn silk tea
Corn starch
Cottage cheese
Cranberries
Cranberry
Cranberry jam
Cream (30% fat)
Cream 10% coffee cream
Cream sour 10%
Cream sour 20%
Cream sour 30%
Creamer
Crispbread
Crucian
Cucumber (bitter)
Cucumber (spicy cucumber)
Currant jam (black)
Currant jam (red)
Currant juice (black)
Currants (black)
Currants (red)
Curry
Curry paste red
Daisy
Dandelion juice
Dashi
Dates red
Deer meat
Deer's Bones
Deer's kidneys
Ducks egg
Dulse (seaweed)
Dyer's broom herb
Edam cheese
Eel smoked
Elderberries
Emmental cheese
Fennel
Fennel seeds ground
Fennel tea
Fenugreek (Trigonella foenum-graecum)
Fernet Branca (herbal bitter liqueur)
Feta cheese
Fish innards
Fish remains
Fish sauce
Flounder
Flower pollen
Fox nut, gorgon nut, makhana
French beans

Fresh cheese from soya
Fresh cheese with herbs
Freshwater crab
Fructose (glucose)
Fruit mix juice
Fruit tea
Gail plum
Galangal
Garam Masala powder
Gelatin white
Gelee Royal
Gentian root
Gentian root tea
Ginger fresh
Ginger powder
Ginkgo fruit
Ginseng
Ginseng liqueur
Ginseng root
Goat and sheep's blood
Goat and sheep's brain
Goat and sheep's liver
Goat and sheep's stomach
Goose blood
Goose fat
Gorgonzola
Gouda cheese
Gourd
Grapefruit dried peel
Grapeseed oil
Grass carp
Green spelt
Greengage
Ground
Ground caraway
Guava
Halibut (Flatfish)
Herbal tea mix
Herbs bitter
Herring
Hibiscus
Hibiscus tea
Hijiki
Hokkaido pumpkin
Honey wine (Met)
Hop
Horehound leaves
Horse meat
Jasmine blossoms tee
Jellyfish
Kaki plum
Kalmus
Kidney beans (red)
King Solomon's-seal

Kohlrabi
Kudzu
Kukicha tea
Ladyfingers
Lamb bones
Lamb kidneys
Lamb liver
Lamb meat
Lamb shoulder
Lamb's lettuce
Lavender blossoms
Leek
Lemon Balm (dried)
Lemon Balm (fresh)
Lemon peel
Lemongrass
Lentils
Lentils black
Lentils red
Lentils yellow
Licorice root tea
Lily bulbs
Lima beans
Lime
Lime blossom tea
Linseed
Linseed (crushed)
Linseed oil
Liver smoothing tea
Loquate / Japanese medlar
Lotus roots
Lotus seeds
Lovage
Lovage seeds
Luo Han Guo fruit
Lychee liqueur
Lye roll
Mackerel
Mango juice
Manioc flour
Mare's milk
Martini
Mascarpone cheese
Mayonnaise 50%
Mayonnaise 80%
Mediterranean fish (cod, plaice,
haddock, sea eel, mackerel)
Medlar
Mirabelle plum
Miso
Miso black (fermented)
Mixed Pickles
Mu Erh Mushroom
Muesli

Mulled Wine Spice
Mullet
Multi-grain bread (gray bread)
Mung bean sprouting
Mustard
Mustard Dijon
Mustard medium hot
Mustard sweet
Nasturtium (nose-twister or nose-tweaker)
Nectarine
Nettles
Noodles (wheat) with egg
Noodles (wheat, lasagne) with egg
Noodles (wheat, ribbon noodles) with egg
Noodles (wheat, spaghetti) with egg
Noodles (whole grain) with egg
Nori, purple seaweed, red algae
Oat
Oat flakes (whole grain)
Oat flour
Oat fusion (baby food)
Oat meal
Oat milk
Octopus
Olives green
Onion (shallot)
Onion (spring onion)
Onion read
Onion white
Orange blossom
Orange dried peel
Orange grated peel
Orange jam
Orange peel
Oregano dried
Oregano fresh
Oyster shell powder
Palm oil
Parsley
Parsley root
Parsnip
Passion blossoms tea
Passion fruit
Peanut (roasted)
Peanut butter
Pearl barley
Pepper powder (hot)
Peppermint tea
Pepperoni
Pepperoni, yellow, pitted, halved
Peppers (sweet)
Peppers powder

Pheasant
Pickle
Pig blood
Pigeon
Pigeon egg
Pinto beans speckled
Plaice
Plum dried
Plums
Pork Bacon
Pork brain
Pork fat (lard)
Pork ham
Pork ham cooked
Pork ham smoked
Pork kidneys
Pork Lard
Pork lung
Pork marrow bones
Pork meat
Pork sausage (Bratwurst) Pork/beef sausage (smoked)
Pork's intestine
Potato (mealy)
Potato flour
Prickly pear
Processed cheese 12%
processed cheese 30%
Prosecco
Psyllium seed
Pudding powder vanilla
Puff pastry
Pumpernickel (dark bread)
Pumpkin
Pumpkin seeds
Quince
Quinoa
Rabbit
Rabbit (wild)
Rabbit liver
Rabbit meat
Radish horseradish
Radish leaves
Raspberry jam
Raspberry leaf tea
Red beet
Red berry (without sugar)
Red cabbage
Ribworttea
Rice (Gaoliang / Sorghum)
Rice mash
Rice starch
Rice sticky
Rice wild (nature rice)

Rose blossom tea
Rose hip
Rose leaf tea
Rosefish
Rosemary
Rum
Rusk
Rye wholemeal bread
Safflower (Dyer's thistle / Hong Hua)
Salmon
Salt
Salt (herbal)
Savory
Savoy cabbage / kale
Sea buckthorn
Sea cucumber
Sesame oil roasted
Sesame paste (Tahini)
Sesame, black
Shark
Sheep's milk yoghurt
Sherry (whine)
Shrimps
Skim milk powder
Slug
Sourdough
Soy noodles
Soy Tofu smoked
Soybean oil
Soybeans, black
Soybeans, blacks, fermented
Spurdog (spiny dogfish, Schillerlocken)
St. Benedict's thistle, blessed thistle,
holy thistle, spotted thistle
Star anise
Stevia (candyleaf, sweetleaf)
Strawberry jam
Sugar - icing sugar
Sugar palm sugar
Sugar substitute (sweetener)
Sunflower seeds
Supplementary nutrition
Sweet potato
Tabasco
Tarragon (Estragon)
Tea mixture uric acid lowering
Thyme
Thyme dried
Toast bread (whole grain)
Tomato dried
Tomato juice
Tomato paste
Tomato puree

Tonic Water
Topinambur
Trout (smoked)
Truffle
Tuna
Turkey ham
Turmeric (yellow root)
Turnip
Turnips
Umeboshi paste
Valerian
Vanilla pod
Vanilla sugar natural
Vinegar Aceto Balsamico white
Walnuts roasted
Water hot
Watermelon
Wax gourd
Wheat flatbread/pita bread
Wheat flour whole grain
Wheat/Rye/Gray-black bread with yeast
Wheatgrass juice
Wheatgrass powder
Whey
White beans
White bread (baguette)
White bread (pretzel sticks)
White bread (roll)
White bread (wheat bread)
White breadcrumbs
White cabbage
White dumpling bread (wheat bread cut
into chunks)
Whitefish
Whole grain bread
Wholemeal flour
Wild boar meat
Wild garlic (garlic spinach)
Wild herbs
Wormwood herb
Yam root, yam root tuber
Yarrow
Yeast
Yew nut
Yoghurt vanilla
Yogi tea
Zucchini

10.2 Use ingredients: yes

Almond
Apple (sour)
Apple (sweet)
Arrowroot
Balm
Barley
Barley not peeled
Bean oil
Black-eyed peas
Blueberry juice
Boletus mushroom
Borage oil
Broccoli
Buckwheat (roasted) Kasha
Bulgur (cereals)
Butter organic
Carrot
Carrot (Early Carrot)
Carrot juice without sugar
Cashews
Cauliflower
Chamomile
Champignon
Chanterelle
Chicken egg
Chicken heart
Chicken liver
Chicken meat
Chicken stomach
Chicken yolk
Chinese cabbage
Coconut grated
Coix (seeds) YiYi Ren
Cooking oil
Corn
Corn Grease (Polenta)
Couscous
Cranberry
Cranberry juice
Currant (black)
Currant (red)
Currant (white)
Elderberry blossom tee
Evening primrose oil
Fig
Fig dried
Freshwater fish
Ginger oil
Goose
Goose parts
Gooseberry

Hawthorn
Hazelnuts
Herbs of Provence
Herbs various
Herbs wild
Lobster
Lychee
Lychee in Preserved
Mallow (Malva sylvestris) blossom tea
Malt
Maple syrup
Margarine
Margarine (diet)
Millet
Millet flakes
Morel (black, dried)
Morel, dried
Nutmeg
Oat flakes roasted
Octopus
Okra
Olive oil
Olives
Oyster mushroom
Peanut oil
Peanuts
Pear
Pear juice
Pearl barley
Peas
Peas, green
Pepperoni, red, pitted, halved
Peppers
Pine nuts
Pistachios
Pork heart
Pork knuckle
Pork liver
Pork skin
Pork stomach
Potato
Pumpkin seed oil
Radish
Radish black
Rapeseed oil
Raspberry dried (immature)
Reishi mushroom
Rice (fragrance)
Rice (whole grain)
Rice Basmati
Rice black

Rice flour
Rice long grain rice
Rice noodles
Rice red
Rice round grain
Rice sweet
Rice variety any
Rye
Rye flour
Saffron
Sage
Salsify
Sauerkraut (cutted cabbage fermented)
Sesame oil
Sesame, white
Shiitake, dried
Sorrel
Sour cherries
Soy flour
Soya Cuisine (soy cream)

Soybean milk
Soybeans
Soybeans, yellow
Spelled (Dark) bread
Spelled flakes
Spelled grain
Spelled semolina
Spelled wholemeal flour
Sugar molasses
Sunflower oil
Tangerine
Thistle oil
Tsampa (roasted barley flour)
Turkey breast meat
Vanilla
Vanilla powder
Vegetable juice
Walnut oil
Water
Wheat germ oil

10.3 Use ingredients: little

Adzuki beans
Almond marzipan
Almond milk
Almond puree
Amaranth
Apricot
Apricots
Artichoke
Asparagus (green or white)
Aubergine
Avocado
Bamboo shoots
Basic recipe for a duck soup
Berry juice
Blackberry´s
Blueberry
Buckwheat
Burdock root tea
Cantaloupe
Carambola (Star fruit)
Carp
Caviar
Cherry juice
Chestnuts
Chives
Clementines
Coconut flakes
Coconut milk
Coffee
Cress

Cumin (Caraway seed)
Dandelion (young plants)
Dandelionroots tea
Dates dried
Deer meat
Dill
Duck (heart)
Duck (slaughtered)
Fish pieces mixed (fresh water)
Fresh cheese
Grape juice red
Grape juice white
Grapefruit (Pomelo)
Grapefruit juice
Grapes red
Grapes white
Honey
Iceberg lettuce
Longane
Marjoram
Mold cheese
Mung bean
Oysters
Peaches
Peaches (canned)
Pepper (ground)
Pepper Cayenne
Pepper white (ground)
Peppercorns
Perch

Pimento
Plum
Pomegranate
Radish (white, green, purple-red)
Raisins
Raspberry
Rhubarb
Rice malt
Rose hip tea
Rucola
Sago (cereals)
Sake
Shrimp
Sour milk cheese 20%
Spinach
Strawberries
Strawberry Juice
Sugar brown
Sugar candy white

Sugar cane sugar
Sugar fructose - fruit sugar
Sugar glucose - grapes sugar
Sugar Milk Sugar
Sugar white
Trout
Vinegar (Apple vinegar)
Vinegar (Red wine vinegar)
Vinegar Aceto Balsamico
Walnuts
Wheat
Wheat bran
Wheat bulgur
Wheat flakes
Wheat flour
Wheat semolina
Wheat semolina for children
Yarrow tea

10.4 Do not use contra-acting foods

Aloe juice
Banana
Banana (cooking banana)
Batavia
Beer (Pils)
Beer (Top-fermented German dark beer)
Black tea
Buttermilk
Chicory
Chlorella (fresh water)
Cow's milk (1.5% fat)
Cow's milk (whole milk 3.5% fat)
Crab
Cream, sweet 30%
Créme fraiche cheese
Cucumber
Curcuma
Curd cheese 20%
Curd cheese 40%
Eel
Endive salad
Feta cheese
Garlic
Goat
Goat and sheep's milk
Goat cheese
Goose egg
Green tea
Hyssop
Juniper berry
Kefir

Kiwi
Kombu seaweed (Saccharina japonica)
Kumquats
Lamb's lettuce
Leaf salads (bitter)
Lemon
Lemon juice
Lettuce
Mango
Mineral water
Miso paste (soy bean paste)
Mozzarella
Mulberry fruit
Mussels
Mustard seeds
Mutton
Mutton
Orange
Orange juice
Papaya
Parmesan
Peppermint
Peppers (rose peppers)
Pineapple
Pineapple (from a can)
Pineapple juice without sugar
Poppy
Quail
Quail egg
Radicchio
Red wine
Romaine lettuce / lettuce salad

Seacrab
Sheep's milk
Sour cream 15% fat
Sour milk
Soy sauce
Soy Tofu
Spiny lobsters
Spirit
Tomato

Umeboshi plums (Japanese apricots)
Wakame
Wheat beer
White wine
Wild strawberries
Wormwood
Yogurt (natural, 1.5% fat)
Yogurt (natural, 3.5% fat)

11 Herbs and their effects

11.1 Basil

thermal effect: warm
taste: spicy, bitter
Dries out, leads down. Tonifies Yang and Qi, dissolves mucus-cold,
eliminates wind-cold.
It has a beneficial effect on flatulence and nausea, relaxing and soothing.
Good to fight emphysema, bronchitis, whooping cough, high blood
pressure, headache, mouth odor, warts, hiccup, gout, migraine.

11.2 Savory

thermal effect: warm
taste: bitter
Tonifies kidney yang, heart qi, stomach and spleen qi and warms the
middle, moves the liver qi and blood, releases mucous and cold from the
lungs, opens the surface, induces wind-cold.
Stomach-strengthening, soothing and appetizing. Ideal for prevent colds,
strengthens the immun system. In case of incontinence or nocturnal
wetting (not for children), put the beans in liquor for libido.

11.3 Nettles

thermal effect: neutral
taste: bitter
Lowers Qi, dries out, direct down. Tonifies Yang, dissolves / transforms
mucus, regulates and moves qi, eliminates wind-cold / heat-wetness.
Promotes urination. Tea or juice, cleanses the blood and the kidneys,
supports prostate problems, inhibit the formation of inflammation, pain-
relieving.

11.4 Coriander

thermal effect: warm
taste: spicy
Driving sweat, reducing wind, draining moisture, tonifying and regulating qi, eliminating wind-cold.
The essential oils are appetizing, digestive, cramping and soothing in stomach and intestinal disorders.

11.5 Herbs various

Stimulates appetite. Effect different.
Appetizing, lots of trace elements and vitamins.

11.6 Cress

thermal effect: cool
taste: sweet
Moves and tonifies qi and blood, diuretic, cools in internal heat, moisturizes lungs, triggers stagnation, heads upwards.
Diuretic, supports urination. Good to fight dry mouth, inner agitation, sore throat, diabetes, kidney stones, gastrointestinal complaints, lung problems, menstrual cramps or cancer.

11.7 Chives

thermal effect: warm
taste: spicy
Directs upward. Tonifies blood, kidney Yang and Qi. Dissolves moisture.
Bactericide, prevents cancer, strengthens gastric juice production, promotes digestion and blood circulation, promotes growth, triggers stagnation.

11.8 Lovage

thermal effect: warm
taste: spicy, bitter
Reduces inner wind and moisture, dissolves stagnation, directs upward, warms Yang, regulates and moves Qi, warms inside, dissolves mucus-cold, eliminates wind-cold.
Stimulates digestion, reduces pain. Extracts of the root are used to flush out urinary tract infections and prevent kidney gravel.

11.9 Lily bulbs

thermal effect: cool
taste: sweet, bitter
Tonifies Yin, soothes Shen / Spirit. Moisturizes the lungs, clears heat and stops coughing.
Calms nerves, good to fight scaly skin. The onions and the petals are added to ointments in the Orient, which can heal muscles and tendons.
White lily (astringent).

11.10   Oregano dried

thermal effect: warm
taste: bitter
Dries out, directs down, regulates and moves Qi, eliminates wind-cold, soothes Shen / Spirit, suppresses inner wind, warms inside, eliminates wind-cold / heat-wetness, moves blood, dissolves slime-cold.
It has an anti-digestive, calming and nerve-strengthening effect, helps to fight cramping stomach and intestinal disorders. The ingredient Carvacrol has an anti-inflammatory effect.

11.11   Parsley

thermal effect: warm
taste: bitter
Nourishes blood and liver, harmonizes liver and spleen, strengthens eyesight, preserves juices, contracts. Dissolves moisture and warms Yang.
Stimulates liver function, detoxifies. Forces urinating. Relieves flatulence. Digestive and menstrual stimulating, birth-accelerating, memory-enhancing, blood-purifying, skin-smoothing.

11.12   Rosemary

thermal effect: warm
taste: bitter
Dries out, leads down. Strengthens the heart, lungs and spleen qi, strengthens liver blood. Strengthens heart-Yin. Expels spleen heat / cold moisture. Strengthens spleen and kidney yang.
Promotes digestion, relieves bloating, strengthens lung, spleen and kidney. Affects the circulation and nerves. Appetizing. Baths help to fight circulatory disorders as well as with gout and rheumatism.

11.13   Sage

thermal effect: neutral
taste: bitter, spicy
Expels slime, guides down, strengthens Qi, eliminates Wind-Heat,
eliminate heat induced by Yin deficiency. Good to fight yeast infections.
The leaves have a digestive effect and are used in greasy foods.
Antiperspirant effect. Helps to relieve coughing attacks. Dries out.

11.14   King Solomon's-seal

thermal effect: neutral
taste: sweet, bitter
Tonifies Yin and Qi, astringent, tonifies blood, eliminates wind-cold / heat-
wetness. Used to repair wounds or damaged tissue. Good to fight dry
cough, earlier also tuberculosis and dysentery, as well as diarrhea and
hemorrhoids.

11.15   Yam root, yam root tuber

thermal effect: neutral
taste: sweet
Tonifies Yin, Yang and Qi, reduces inner wind, dissolves wetness, warms
Yang. Solves cramps (in the gastrointestinal tract). Digestive through
increased bile production. Anti-inflammatory in rheumatic diseases.
Mucolytic agent for coughing. Relief of menopausal symptoms.

11.16   Lemongrass

thermal effect: taste:
Diverting, calming.
Reduction of flatulence, antimicrobial, appetizing. Prevention of influenza.
Good to fight infections in the mouth and throat.

11.17   Lemon Balm (fresh)

thermal effect: cool
taste: sour
Soothes Shen / Spirit, regulates and moves Qi, eliminates heat caused
by Yin deficiency, tones Qi. Stimulating, antibacterial, encouraging,
relaxing, antispasmodic, cooling, antipyretic, analgesic, sweat-inducing,
virus-inhibiting. Good for colds, fever, flu, cough, bronchitis, asthma, loss
of appetite, bloating, heartburn.

12 Basics of Nutrition

The basic principles of nutrition described herein are general recommendations. They are not aimed at a specific form of therapy. Recommendations concerning a therapy have priority.

12.1 Nutrition

Regular meals in a relaxed atmosphere. A warm breakfast is considered a good start into the day.
The main meals ought to be taken for lunch – supper in the early evening. Pay attention to feeling hungry or sated: don't eat too much nor remain hungry is the rule
Prepare the meals freshly from natural, regional products. Frozen, heat-conserved, industrially prepared or foodstuffs cooked in the microwave oven are rejected.
Choice of foodstuffs according to the season: more cooling food in summer, more warming food in winter.
Eat cooked food at least twice a day. Food and drinks ought to be lukewarm, never ice-cold or hot.
Raw vegetables, briefly cooked vegetables, freshly squeezed juices and mineral water are not recommended. Milk and dairy products are only included in the diet if they don't cause problems. Don't use therapeutic recipes over a longer period without consulting your doctor or therapist.

Varied food
Enjoy the diversity of foodstuffs. Characteristics of a balanced nutrition are variety, suitable combination and a balanced quantity of rich and low energy foodstuffs (on one hand avoiding undersupply with essential nutrients and on the other hand to take to many undesirable substances).

A lot of Cereal Products - and Potatoes
Bread, pasta, rice, cereal flakes (best wholemeal) as well as potatoes contain almost no fat, but many vitamins, mineral nutrients, trace elements, roughage and secondary plant substances. These foodstuffs ought to be taken with low-fat side dishes.

Vegetables and Fruit – „Take Five" every day … 5 portions of vegetables and fruit a day, as fresh as possible, briefly cooked, or maybe one portion as a juice – ideal as a side dish to every meal as well as snack between meals: Thus a lot of vitamins, mineral nutrients as well as roughage and secondary plant substances

Daily milk and dairy products
Milk and Dairy Products every Day, once or twice per Week Fish; meat, sausages as well as eggs moderately. These foodstuffs contain valuable nutrients like calcium in the milk, iodine selenium and omega-3 fat acids in saltwater fish. Meat is favorable due to its high content of disposable iron and the vitamins B1, B6 and B12. Quantities of 300 – 600 g meat and sausage per week are sufficient. Prefer low-fat products, especially in meat- and dairy products.

Low-fat and fatty Foodstuffs
Fat supplies us with essential fat acids and fatty foodstuffs contain also fat-soluble vitamins. Fat is high in energy; therefore much fat in the food may cause overweight, possibly also cancer. Too many saturated fat acids may further a tendency for cardio-vascular diseases in the long term. Prefer vegetable oils and fats (e.g. rapeseed-, olive-, soya-oils and solid fats produced therefrom). Beware of invisible fat in meat- and dairy products, pastry and sweets as well as in fast-food and convenience foods. 70 – 90 g fat per day is sufficient.

Moderately Sugar and Salt
Take sugar and foods/drinks containing various kinds of sugar (e.g. glucose syrup) only occasionally. Use herbs and spices as well as a little salt creatively. Prefer salt containing iodine.

Plenty of Liquids
Water is absolutely essential. Drink 1-2 l liquids every day. Prefer water (with or without gas) and other low-calorie drinks. Alcoholic drinks should not be taken.

Tasty Dishes, carefully cooked
Cook the meals with as low temperatures and as short as possible, using little water and fat – this preserves the original taste, keeps the nutrients intact and prevents the production of harmful compounds.

Take time and enjoy the food
Take your Time and enjoy your Food
Eating consciously helps to eat right. The eye enjoys food, too. It's fun, invites to enjoy varied dishes and stimulates the feeling of satiety.

Watch your Weight and stay in Motion
A balanced diet and a lot of exercise and sport (30 – 60 min/day) are a healthy combination. The right weight furthers well-being and health. Thermals, directional effectiveness, digestive power

There are various criteria for judging the effectiveness of herbs and foodstuffs.

The use of certain herbs and ingredients is based on observations of the effects on the body which these foodstuffs, herbs and spices show after having eaten them. The medical science has developed following system: Every ingredient or herb has a directional effectiveness. Furthermore, there are herbs which have a special effect on certain organs.

The basic condition for a healthy metabolism is to obtain sufficient energy from food and that the digestive process doesn't use too much energy. An easily digestible meal makes content and sated, doesn't cause flatulence and fatigue after the meal. The perfect spices increase the healthiness of our meals. Very often, just small doses of herbs and spices will suffice. They are not used to make us sated, but to help our digestive organs to digest the food.

12.2 Recipes

The recipes list the ingredients to be used and the cooking instructions show how the dish is prepared. The list of ingredients shows the concerned quantities as well as the relevance for the therapy. If you find „less than mentioned", try to comply or find an alternative from the „list of recommended foodstuffs". Mostly it shall result just in a small change of taste when you simply avoid this ingredient.

Mild cooking methods: boiling, stewing, poaching, steaming
Strong cooking methods: barbecuing, roasting, frying, smoking
Balanced cooking methods: deep-frying, baking brick
Deep-freezing and warming in the microwave oven should be avoided (denaturalization).

12.3 Foodstuffs

Foodstuffs have an effect on body and soul like medicinal herbs, only a very much milder one. Dietary advice is mainly based on regional foodstuffs. The knowledge about the effects of each foodstuff and the knowledge, when which foodstuff shall be used, is based on the orthodox school of medicine. Use ecologic-organic products, if possible. As everything should be cooked for a long time due to a better digestability and very rarely eaten raw, the food agrees with everyone.

The classification of the foodstuffs according to their effect on the body is the basis in order to achieve a harmonious status of health.

Dietary advisors do not recommend certain foodstuffs for everyone. The individual diet is tailor-made for the individual constitution.

Buy only fresh and ripe fruit and vegetables. You ought to leave unripe fruit and vegetables and such with brown spots and wilted leaves behind in the market. In this case take deep-frozen goods (never ready-to-serve dishes!). Fruit and vegetables are deep-frozen immediately after harvesting and often contain more vitamins and minerals than the goods from the vegetable shelf. Whereas conserved or tinned goods contain very much less biological substances. Also, salt, sugar and others are mostly added to the latter. Never leave the foodstuffs in the water after washing them to avoid that many vital substances get drowned. Clean salads, fruit and vegetables immediately before serving.

Please make sure of the hygienic processing of foodstuffs. Clean your salads, fruit and vegetables carefully. When cooking with meat, prepare all ingredients first and then process the meat products. Clean the worktop and tools very carefully. Wooden surfaces ought to be treated with a mild disinfectant regularly in order to reduce germination. Store fruit and vegetables separately, if possible. Harvested fruit and vegetables are still alive and emit e.g. ethylene gas, which makes other products ripen and age faster. Keep meat and fish in the closed packaging or store them in the fridge in closed containers.

12.4 Herbs

There are some basic rules for storing medicinal herbs. On principle, herbs must be protected from direct sunlight, humidity and heat.

Containers for the storage of herbs may be glasses, ceramic jars and even plastic containers. However, plastic is a rather unsuitable material and should only be a short-term solution. In case of glass containers, use a dark material.

Medicinal herbs cannot be kept for any long period. The shelf life of herbs is limited. However, it can be prolonged with suitable storage. The place should be dark, rather cool and absolutely dry. A wooden medicine cabinet, placed not directly next to a source of heat, would be ideal. Never buy large quantities of herbs so as not to have to throw them away. Label the container with the name of the herb and the date of harvesting or processing.

13 Other dietic-books

The following syndromes of dietetics, TCM or for a therapy supplement for cancer are available.

<u>Dietetics</u>
E001. Nutrition of the infant - baby food
E002. Nutrition during lactation
E003. Nutrition in old age
E004. Nutrition of children and adolescents
E005. Nutrition of athletes
E006. Light weight
E007. Pregnancy
E008. Full food

Protein and electrolyte - kidneys
E009. (hemodialysis) dialysis treatment
E010. Acute renal failure
E011. Chronic renal insufficiency
E012. Nephrotic syndrome
E013. Kidney stones (nephrolithiasis)

Gastrointestinal tract - pancreas
E014. Acute pancreatitis (inflammation of the pancreas)
E015. Chronic pancreatitis (inflammation of the pancreas)

Gastrointestinal tract - small intestine and large intestine
E016. Acute obstipation (constipation)
E017. Chronic obstipation (constipation)
E018. Colon irritabile
E019. Diverticulitis
E020. Acquired lactose intolerance (lactose malabsorption)
E021. Fructose malabsorption
E022. Glutensensitive enteropathy (celiac disease)
E023. Colectomy
E024. Short Bowel Syndrome

Gastrointestinal tract - liver, gallbladder, bile ducts
E025. Acute and chronic hepatitis (inflammation of the liver)
E026. Cholelithiasis (bile stones)
E027. fatty liver
E028. cirrhosis

Gastrointestinal tract - Stomach and duodenal intestine
E029. Acute gastritis
E030. Chronic gastritis
E031. Stomach bleeding
E032. Ulcus ventriculi and duodenal ulcer
E033. Condition after gastric surgery

Gastrointestinal tract - oral cavity and esophagus
E034. Stomatitis
E035. Esophageal carcinoma (esophageal cancer)
E036. Refluosophagitis (heartburn)

Special diseases
E037. Phenylketonuria (PKU)
E038. Rheumatic joint diseases

Metabolism
E039. Obesity (overweight)
E040. Diabetes mellitus
E041. Eating disorders (underweight)

Fat metabolism
E042. Hypercholesterolaemia (increased cholesterol level)
E043. Hepatic Encephalopathy

Heart and circulation
E044. Arteriosclerosis (arterial calcification)
E045. Heart insufficiency
E046. Hypertension
E047. Hyperuricaemia and gout

Changed nutrient requirements
E048. In case of fever
E049. For malignant diseases
E050. After burns
E051. Radiation and chemotherapy

CANCER
E100. Pancreatic cancer
E101. Bladder cancer
E102. Blood cancer (leukemia)
E103. Breast cancer
E104. Colorectal cancer
E105. Gastric cancer
E106. Kidney cancer
E107. Esophageal cancer

TCM
E200. Bladder - moisture heat in the bladder
E201. Bladder - moisture and cold in the bladder
E202. Bladder - emptiness and cold in the bladder
E203. Large intestine - external cold affects the large intestine
E204. Large intestine - moisture heat in the large intestine
E205. Large intestine - heat blocks the intestine II acute
E206. Large intestine - dryness of the colon
E207. Large intestine - Yang deficiency (cold)
E208. Heart - Blood insufficiency
E209. Heart - Blood stagnation
E210. Heart - Fire
E211. Heart - Hot mucus clogs the heart pores

E212. Heart - Cold mucus clogs the heart pores
E213. Heart - Qi deficiency
E214. Heart - Yang deficiency
E215. Heart - Yin deficiency
E216. Liver - Ascending Liver Yang
E217. Liver - Blood deficiency
E218. Liver - Blood stagnation
E219. Liver - Moisture heat in liver and gall bladder
E220. Liver - Fire
E221. Liver - Gall bladder Qi-Empty
E222. Liver - Cold in the liver meridian
E223. Liver - Qi stagnation
E224. Liver - Wind
E225. Liver - Wind with ascending liver Yang
E226. Liver - Wind with blood anemic
E227. Liver - Wind with extreme heat
E228. Lung - Qi deficiency
E229. Lung - Mucus-moisture in the lungs
E230. Lung - Mucus-heat in the lungs
E231. Lung - Mucus-cold in the lungs
E232. Lung - Dryness of the lungs
E233. Lung - Wind-heat attacks the lungs
E234. Lung - Wind-cold affects the lungs
E235. Lung - Yin deficiency
E236. Stomach - Bloodstagnation
E237. Stomach - Fire
E238. Stomach - Cold with liquid
E239. Stomach - Nutrition stagnation
E240. Stomach - Qi deficiency
E241. Stomach - Rebellious Qi
E242. Stomach - Yin Emptiness
E243. Spleen - Heat and moisture attack the spleen
E244. Spleen - Coldness and moisture affects the spleen
E245. Spleen - Qi deficiency
E246. Spleen - Qi deficiency + Declining spleen Qi
E247. Spleen - Qi deficiency + spleen does not control the blood
E248. Spleen - Yang deficiency
E249. Kidney - Heart and kidney no longer communicate
E250. Kidney - Jing deficiency
E251. Kidney - Kidneys cannot receive the Qi
E252. Kidney - Qi is not stable
E253. Kidney - Yang deficiency
E254. Kidney - Yin deficiency

For further information visit di-book.com.